BREAKING AND TRAINING THE STOCK HORSE

By *Charles O. Williamson*

CHARLES O. WILLIAMSON, D. V. M.

Silhouettes by James Wallis
Sketches by Carl Hoobing

Printed and bound in the United States of America by
The CAXTON PRINTERS, Ltd.
Caldwell, Idaho
70566

To
Range Men Everywhere

CONTENTS

FOREWORD

Since horse training requires deep thought and an endless amount of patience, plus skill and tact, it is imperative that you possess or develop the necessary traits before you can be successful at this work. It is said that quite a large percentage of people refuse to read anything of depth because they do not wish to make the mental effort necessary to think deeply. If you are one of this group or, if you are one of those who say you could never get anything out of reading, you can learn better by just "doing"; if you do not have the patience to *continually repeat and seemingly get little result* from your efforts, it is much better that you start to train yourself first.

In assembling this set of instructions on horse training and horsemanship, effort has been made to eliminate all unnecessary words and sentences. Therefore, in its application, it is necessary that strict attention be paid to each and every statement. Failure to do so may mean failure in training your horse.

To derive any benefit from this course in horsemanship, it must be followed from the beginning because the first lessons are the most important. They contain the fundamental principles of horse training and lay the groundwork for the final results for which the course is intended. For instance, a horse cannot be taught to stop properly and turn on his hind feet until he has first been suppled and made light and taught to respond instantly to the use of hands and legs.

Forget the old idea that because someone "has been around horses all his life" he is sure to be a good horseman. Such is by no means the case. Many of these good people are very poor horsemen and admit it, while others feel free to offer much advice.

Do not think that all people who make their living handling cattle on horseback are good horsemen, much less all those who wear so-called Western clothes and use so-called Western riding equipment and perhaps occasionally help drive a bunch of gentle cattle somewhere or chase a calf in an arena. Many of the real ones are poor horsemen and many of those who are good horsemen ride in shoes and very much dislike a pair of chaps (chaparejos) which they never wear except for good reasons such as cold weather or for riding through thick brush. If you wish to appear rough and tough and keep your horse afraid of you and in a lather much of the time; if you wish to teach him to rear and walk on his hind legs (any mechanic can do it), it would be best if you gave this book to someone who is interested in horsemanship such as is practiced by a few men of the ranges.

Pay no attention to the old "wheeze," "Well, some people train horses one way and some another." All real trainers of saddle horses work above all things for the fundamental principle of lightness in their horses, even if they do not call it by that name. After this is obtained, horses may be taught almost anything. If you will stick it out and follow these instructions and make just one horse light, you will realize the full meaning of the word and forever after will frown upon such crude practices as shoeing a horse behind and rasping down his front feet until they are tender, in order to *make* him stop on his hind feet; working him against a fence to *make* him turn; using severe bits in order to *hold* him; and other similar practices.

All horses are two-sided as far as training is concerned. What you teach on one side means nothing to the horse when the same indications are used on the other side. Therefore, it is necessary to teach everything from both sides.

Remember that when considering horsemanship, the use of weights, ropes, and other mechanical devices such as bitting rigs, tie-downs, tying a horse's head to one side to "limber up his neck," and other such practices are mechanics and not horsemanship and have no place in a course of this kind. Use of such practices makes a horse still more mechanical in his movements and if he ever "limbers up" it is through hard usage and then the horse learns it in spite of the rider, not with his help.

The teaching of tricks is not horsemanship in the strict

sense of the word, although it is not objectionable if done without abuse. A well-trained trick horse is a pleasure to watch perform. Tricks have nothing to do with fine riding. Do not make the mistake of referring to a trick or a circus horse as a high school horse. Such reference is very erroneous as high school riding represents the highest type of horsemanship.

It should go without saying that no one without a certain amount of tact and a leaning in that direction can ever meet with much success at horse training and the same can be said for any other kind of specialized work. However, any horse lover could learn to ride and handle horses fairly efficiently if he would only apply himself.

There are a few facts concerning horses which have always been unexplainable to me. One is that an untrained horse, when mounted, and often even on the halter, wants to turn on his front feet but when loose in a pasture always turns on his hind feet. Another is that any horse, even a hard-mouthed, spoiled horse, will eventually become light on the bit and light to some degree in action by the continued, proper use of hands and legs. Of course there are many riders who are always ready and willing to offer an explanation for these phenomena but I have never heard one that satisfies me.

It requires an endless amount of patience to train horses but it also requires something else. It requires skill and tact. A great many people talk as if patience were the only requisite.

Do not rush the horse in any period of his training. After all, a few weeks or even months in the training period is but a short time in the life of the horse and there should be no hurry. In case a horse becomes stale in his training and "sours," he should be left alone for several days, or at most, ridden casually.

When following the instructions in this course there will be times when it seems certain that parts of it cannot possibly be correct but if you will persist and have patience you will win out in the long run.

Read and re-read these instructions. As with any set of instructions, you will see something each time which you failed to see before.

After the instructions on breaking, do not attempt to follow any other part of this course until you have carried out the instructions on suppling a horse and making him light. Lightness is the basis of all good saddle horse training.

The author of this course in horsemanship and training has spent the greater part of his life in a saddle and many years on the remote ranges. He has made an intensive study of horse nature and the things that cause a horse to respond to training and feels competent to offer the advice and instructions set forth herein.

GENERAL REMARKS ON HORSEMANSHIP

GOOD HORSEMANSHIP requires a large amount of tact. This word, tact, includes many things and one of the main things is knowing when to pull and when to slack when handling a horse. Make it a rule to stay slack most of the time, whether you are teaching a colt to lead, leading him afterward, riding him, or holding a nervous horse for any purpose. This is very important. You cannot have success with this course unless you remember it *all the time you are working*.

A horse responds to training to relieve pressure on some part of his body. He follows you when you are leading him to relieve pressure on his poll. He goes forward when the legs are used to relieve pressure on his sides. He stops or slows when the reins are pulled backward to relieve pressure on his mouth. When he does what you want, if you do not slack and relieve pressure, he has no incentive to do the same thing again for you and finally gives up in disgust and carries you about in a "don't-care" or even a defiant manner because he must. Many horses become unmanageable until handled by different methods. Details appear under the different sections of the course.

Another thing to remember is that a good horseman does not *make* nor *force* his horse to perform. He teaches the fundamentals of the use of the hands, legs, and body and the horse performs willingly at the slightest indication of these aids, whether it be a sliding stop on hind feet, fast reining, or an intricate movement of high school. For that reason, severe bits and sharp spurs are hindrances rather than helps and especially in spoiled horses.

Also remember that being able to ride a bucking horse does not constitute horsemanship. If you can ride him on balance and not on a "death grip" with the legs and a "death pull" on the reins, that is a necessary part of horsemanship, a good seat, but it is only a small part. No credit is due anyone for being able to *hold* himself on a bucking horse by sheer strength of legs and arms. A horse seldom bucks with a good horseman and especially if he has trained the horse himself.

RIDING

No one can become a good horse trainer nor ride and properly handle a good horse unless he is capable of sticking on under almost any and all circumstances. In other words, he must have a good seat in a saddle. To acquire a good seat he must have a reasonably good natural sense of balance in the first place. A good rider rides on balance, not on grip, and even when the going is rough and there are "fireworks," little grip should be necessary.

The Seat,
or
Sticking On

The type of saddle is not too important although it is hard to acquire good balance in deep saddles with high forks and cantles and especially in stock saddles with raised seats in front. The raise prevents the rider from getting "down" and forward in the seat when there is action in order to bring his center of gravity directly over the center of gravity of the horse. The center of gravity of the rider is in the region of the diaphragm above the stomach; that of the horse is directly back of the shoulders and about the middle of the body from top to bottom. When riding leisurely in a walk, it is natural and correct to sit back in the seat of the saddle, but, even when trotting, the seat should be forward and more on the crotch than on the buttocks. This makes it easier for both horse and rider.

When riding in a walk, the weight of the legs only should be on the heels, so that the latter are a little lower than the toes. Let the legs assume a natural position. If the toes are inclined to turn outward, let them. If they point straight forward that is all right. Pictures of the finest riders in the world, at the Olympic Games, riders of high jumpers, often show feet turned at almost right angles to the horse's body. Riders who sit back in the seat of the saddle with feet thrust forward and who depend entirely on a vise-like grip of the legs and the riding of halter or hackamore rein to keep them on when the going is rough should not be copied. Such

The correct seat. Sitting straight up, back concave, sitting on crotch rather than on buttocks, heels down and back of perpendicular.

methods do not constitute good riding. They cannot be followed for more than short periods at one time.

The rider should be relaxed and should practice for a good posture with head up, shoulders squared away, *back concave*, so as to tilt the pelvis forward and put him on the crotch. If the novice is not tense but rides in relaxed ease, he will not become sore and stiff even from his first ride.

When riding at gaits faster than a walk, not only the weight of the legs but half of the weight of the body, should be on the heels, *the muscles of the legs relaxed*, thus bringing the heels much lower than the toes. Thus the rider more or less "floats" on the saddle. The jar of the horse is thus taken and distributed in the ankles, the knees, the crotch, and the waist and amounts to nothing. The faster the gait, the farther forward the body should be leaned, the knees well forward, and the *heels well back of perpendicular*, by all means not out in front. The seat just described is generally known as the "forward seat," and is usually frowned upon by riders of gaited horses which are ridden almost altogether in the show ring and which, because of this fact, do not require too much balance, but all good riders of hunters and jumpers and men doing actual hard riding on the ranges (not rodeo riders), use this seat when the going is rough. It is seen exclusively at the Olympic games where there are no gaited horses nor bucking horses. *It is the balanced seat.* Much practice is required to acquire this seat and especially if you have already learned other ways of riding but if you once master it, you will use no other and will not be tossed over the horse's head if he suddenly stops and whirls or refuses a jump, or plays up, or suddenly kicks very high. When learning and practicing for the balanced seat, do not be surprised and discouraged if, for awhile, it seems very impractical and difficult to acquire. Some day you will find yourself using it unconsciously and ridng easily and after that no effort will be necessary to maintain it.

Range men and riders of hunters and jumpers, for the most part, ride with their feet "home" in the stirrups; that is, the stirrup is against the heel of the boot or shoe. It is better for the amateur to ride with the ball of the foot in the stirrup or, better still, just back of the ball, with heels well down, of course. When the term, "heels well down," is used, it is not meant that the heels are down as a result of using muscles to turn up the toes but rather that the *ankles are entirely relaxed* and the heels are down from weight of the body.

For leisurely riding, the stirrups may be long; for ordinary hill riding, and for hacking, they should be shorter so that, in a stock saddle, the seat may be raised two inches off the saddle when standing in the stirrups; and for fast or rough riding, they should be real short. However, if you ride a stock saddle, you probably do not want to be continually changing the length of the stirrups so set them at medium length and leave them.

If a young rider will learn and practice the method of riding outlined above, he may, in a not-too-lengthy period of time ride the average bucking horse out of a chute in an English saddle or a low roper and fan him with the hat. He cannot scratch with the spurs in the horse's shoulders but neither will he be compelled to ride the halter rein nor grip excessively with the legs in order to stay on. Riding forward in the seat and with weight on the heels, ankles relaxed, the rider feels as if his legs were wrapped around the horse and he needs no grip. Practice this seat at all times when in action. If you will examine the pictures of early day riders on the range by Remington and Russell, you will see that those riders used the seat described above and did not sit back on the horse's loins with feet thrust forward nor ride the reins when "fireworks" started. Riding of the reins, on a bucking horse was the basis for much "ribbing" among early day range riders. Nothing takes the place of daily practice in acquiring a good seat on a horse.

If the amateur wishes and expects to be worthy of the name of *horseman* instead of being a mere rider who may sit on a rough horse and "steer him out and steer *Hands, Legs* him back," it is absolutely necessary that he *and Body* develop light hands and strong decisive legs which he uses continually, and that he learn the importance of the shifting of the body weight in controlling the movements of his horse. The term, light hands, is a little hard to define. It has nothing to do with the actual weight or size of the hands but refers more to the way in which they are used. Ride with arms relaxed and close to the sides; no "flapping" of the elbows as if they were wings. Keep a soft, flexible wrist and flexible fingers. Never pull a steady pull on a horse's mouth; instead, use something of a tremor in the hands and fingers—when you check or stop, when reining to right or left, when backing. Practice this until it is second nature to you and you are not conscious of doing it. Ride much on a slack rein. *Every time your horse responds and does what you want and indicate, slack immediately, any time, anywhere,* perhaps imperceptibly to anyone watching, but slack, nevertheless. The horse will respond again to induce you to slack again. When travelling forward, if your horse is going too fast and you wish to slow, pull and slack, pull and slack (a tremor of the hand), until he slows to the desired speed, then slack and ride on a slightly loose rein until he speeds too fast again. After repeating this process a few times, he usually decides to maintain the speed at which you set him in order to induce you to ride with slack in the rein. Riding on a loose rein does not mean that the reins are hanging with a foot or more of slack in them but that there is no pressure on the horse's mouth. Only a small amount of slack in the rein is necessary or desirable.

This principle of slacking at the right time is a large part of horsemanship. Use it constantly. When riding and a stop is made, slack immediately so that the horse may rest his mouth. Never sit with reins so tight as to prevent the horse from having an absolutely free head. When leading a horse which has been taught properly to lead at your side, you walking at his shoulder, never allow the weight of your hand and arm to hang on the bridle or halter rein. It is a sign of heavy, careless hands. To be a successful horseman, the matter of "hands" must be mastered.

After a horse has been trained properly, legs and body are more important than hands, as a trained horse is ridden chiefly with the legs and body even to reining and backing. Learn to use the legs constantly. *Do not kick. Squeeze* from the thigh to the ankle, most of the pressure coming at the calves. The idea in squeezing the horse is to keep him on the bit. If he is not on the bit, he is not collected and you have little control over him. Of course, in riding across country, collection is not desired and the horse should be allowed to extend himself.

When training, it is necessary to squeeze at almost every other step but the farther along you advance, the less squeezing is necessary because the horse has learned to stay on the bit and also responds more quickly to the use of the legs. When well trained, he responds instantly to the slightest indication from the legs. Unless you have had experience in training horses, at first it will seem that you are getting nowhere with squeezing your horse since many good horses do not respond at all; but, in a couple of weeks, if you give a lesson every day, you will begin to notice that the hind legs immediately "shoot" forward when you squeeze and especially if you use occasional light taps of the squirt at the time of the squeeze. He responds to the squeeze to avoid the tap of the quirt.

A squeeze from the legs should be the first indication for any movement, even for backing. The squeeze puts him on his toes and ready for the next indication, whatever it may be. The horse should be taught to stand for mounting (see elsewhere) and to remain standing until the legs close on his body. If you rein to the *right*, use the *left* leg and lean your body to the right; if to the *left*, use the *right* leg, and lean your body to the left. Use the legs *with heels down* and do not try to touch the horse with the heels. The reason for this is made apparent in that portion of these instructions which deals with suppling. If you ride with the correct position as described above, the legs will always be close to the horse's side. After a while, the horse will rein on the legs and body alone without use of reins and the same is true for backing which will be dealt with elsewhere.

Use the legs against the horse's body *right where they hang in the stirrups*, which is just back of the cinch. He learns to respond quicker and better when they are used there. *Do not use them backward toward the horse's flank.* This irritates him. *Never kick except in emergencies.* A well trained horse will jump far and suddenly when kicked.

Do not underestimate the use of the body in good riding. The finest horsemen in the world ride their *trained* horses chiefly by shifting the weight of their bodies, to a smaller extent with their legs, and practically nil with the reins. It is possible you have seen a high school horse or a stock horse perform without a bridle. There is nothing mysterious about this. The horse has simply been trained to respond to the use of body and legs until hands and reins are not necessary. A cutting horse that works "on his own" without training other than practice in handling cattle is not an example. This horse works because he likes to work and takes to it naturally; not because of training. He will turn a cow in spite of his rider and all credit must go to the horse. With proper training, many horses *become* good cutting horses that otherwise would be suitable only for ordinary riding.

Learning to ride almost entirely by use of the body (shifting of weight) is within reach of only a few but you should not be content until you have learned to ride and train a horse so that you ride him with body and legs and with only slight use of the reins.

Do not use spurs until after a horse is trained. If spurs are used constantly during the uncertain training period, he pays no special attention to them by the time he is finished. If used after the training period, many horses respond doubly quick. Only an experienced trainer is capable of using spurs correctly in the process of training and I disapprove of them even in his case. A lazy horse will eventually learn to respond quickly to the use of the legs if you have patience and follow the instructions given above.

By tact is meant that sixth sense which good horsemen acquire which tells them to do or not to do certain things.

Tact For instance, a good horseman does not look a nervous or dangerous horse directly in the eye but makes it appear that he *knows* everything is going to be all right. The horse also usually gets the same idea. When riding a nervous horse which likes to play and act as if he is afraid of certain objects such as trucks, newspapers, and the like he does not tighten the reins but *slacks* and whistles or sings and uses the legs lightly. If the horse whirls, he appears calm and uses the reins only casually. As a result the horse soon quits such antics. A person, and it is not always a man, who possesses this sixth sense, or tact, may often accomplish uncanny things with horses; that is, they appear uncanny to those who do not have it. It is acquired by much thinking about horse nature and by incessant practice in handling horses. Some seem never to acquire it while others seem almost to be born with it.

TRAINING EQUIPMENT

Contrary to the usual idea, *little* equipment is necessary in the proper training of saddle horses. It consists of

1. THE HACKAMORE OR CAVESON. If the former is used (and I prefer it) the mecate or lead rope should be 18 to 20 feet in length so that it may be used as a longe line. The bosal should be of large diameter, 5/8" or even 3/4", with heavy heel knot and preferably tapered nose button. If a caveson is used, the longe (not lunge) line should be of light material such as 1/4" sash cord or a light web line 20 feet

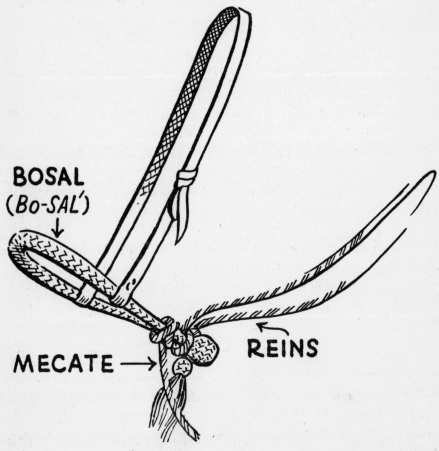

BOSAL
(Bo-SAL')

MECATE →

← REINS

The Hackamore (La Jáquima)

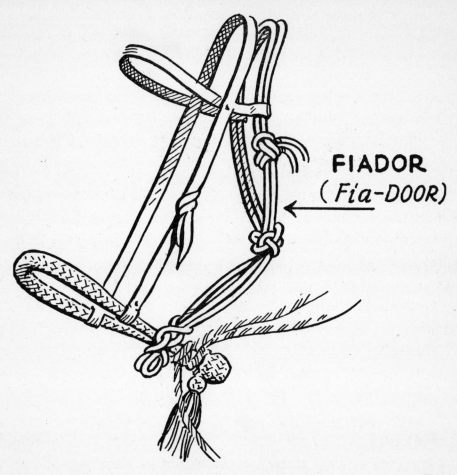

FIADOR
(*Fía-DOOR*)

The Hackamore with Fiador (Not the Theodore)
(La Jáquima con Fiador)

in length. In the following instructions, when the term longe
line is used, reference is made to the mecate or hackamore
lead rope.

2. TWO WHIPS. These are needed but are not absolutely
necessary. A driving (buggy) whip, 6 or 7 feet long, is
very convenient when working the horse on the longe but
a willow switch or a piece of rope may be used to start the
horse if a whip is not available. Much judgment must be used
with anything resembling a whip. Teach your horse to respect
a whip and respond to it; never to fear it.

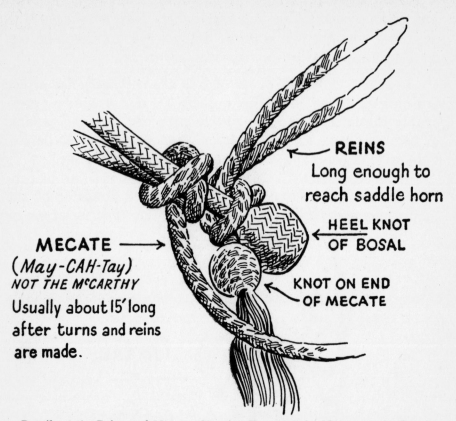

REINS
Long enough to
reach saddle horn

**HEEL KNOT
OF BOSAL**

**KNOT ON END
OF MECATE**

MECATE ⟶
(May-CAH-Tay)
NOT THE M°CARTHY
Usually about 15´long
after turns and reins
are made.

Details of the Reins and Mecate. Showing Turns of the Mecate on the Bosal.

A short, *stiff* quirt, 24 to 30 inches long, when used correctly and sensibly in training often helps to secure and hold attention when the legs alone fail. It should be used seldom and lightly across the shoulders and only to gain attention; *never for punishment.* Each time the quirt is used for attention the legs should be used strongly first. The horse will then learn to respond to legs quicker to avoid the tap of the quirt. Limber quirts and quirts with lashes on the ends should not be used. A limber quirt is too slow and a quirt with a lash often produces a wrong effect.

3. THE BRIDLE. A light, plain bridle is to be preferred. Why cover up a horse's head with a heavy bridle and especially if it is a pretty head? The reins especially should be light. I prefer ½″ reins. Heavy reins may ruin a light mouth

and make a head-tosser or a star-gazer. Never tie a horse to anything with the bridle reins. Use the hackamore, a halter, or a neck rope.

4. BITS. Only two types of bits are necessary for either training or riding of horses; namely the bar or snaffle (preferably the latter) and the simple curb bit. Anyone capable of using a severe bit of any description needs no such device. Others, in my opinion, should not be allowed to use one.

There are no particular measurements which can be considered best for a snaffle bit. The average diameter of the mouth piece at the ring is about ⅜", but if it is larger or

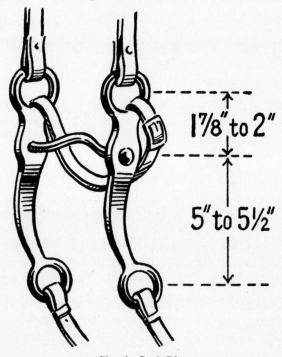

1⅞" to 2"

5" to 5½"

Simple Curb Bit

smaller it makes little difference if you use good judgment and light hands.

In a curb bit the important measurement is the distance on the cheek from the center of the bar (mouthpiece) to the center of the ring or opening into which the headstall is inserted. This distance should be two inches, not more, and

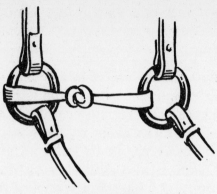

Snaffle Bit

not under 1⅞ inches. It governs the effectiveness of the bit, together with the tightness or looseness of the curb strap.

The length of the shank (that portion of the cheek of the bit from the mouthpiece down) of the curb bit is not too important if the rider uses light hands. However, the ideal length seems to be about 5 or 5½″. The longer the shank the lighter the hands must be in order not to produce the wrong effect.

The port or raise in the center of the mouthpiece should be low, or there should be none at all.

The adjustment of the bridle in the case of either the snaffle or the curb bit is important. The bit should fit snugly into the corners of the mouth. It should not be so high as to wrinkle the skin or low enough to leave a space. The lower the bit the more severe it is.

In the case of the curb bit, the curb strap should be adjusted so that it fits snugly against the lower jaw of the horse. A common mistake is to leave this strap too loose and this causes the corners of the mouth to be pinched between the strap and the bit every time the reins are used. This fact is easily demonstrated. This is the cause of nervousness and fretting in many good saddle horses. Small sores will usually be found at the corners of their mouths.

Everything can be done with a snaffle bit that can be done with a curb bit, but in the case of a light-handed rider the curb bit is very efficient in inducing the horse to relax the muscles of the lower jaw. In the case of a heavy-handed rider, it is much better if it were never used until he learns to use his hands differently.

5. THE SADDLE. It is almost impossible to train a horse properly in a saddle with heavy stirrup leathers which hinder and almost prevent the correct use of the legs. That is why most horse trainers use English, or English type saddles. A surcingle with stirrups would do as well. The old cavalry saddle, the McClellan, is also suitable since it allows the legs to come in close contact with the horse. The same is true for Mexican saddles. After a horse is trained well, any kind of a saddle may be used, since he responds to the slightest pressure from the legs.

A good plan is to ride the green colt (according to in-

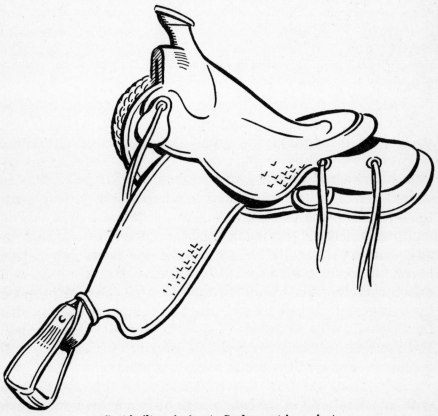

Seat built up in front. Such a seat is against
the principles of good riding.

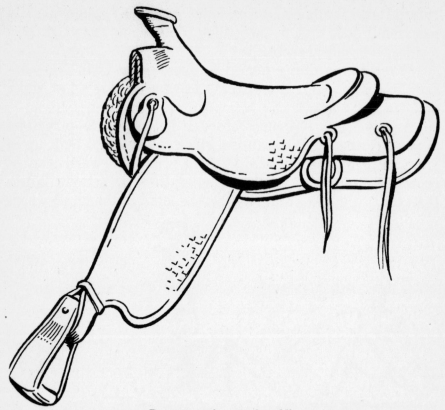

Proper seat in a stock saddle

structions) for 10 days or two weeks, or until he has all notions of fighting out of his head, with a stock saddle, then change to an English type or remove the fenders from a stock saddle and use that through the training period; or use a surcingle with stirrups. An English type saddle or a surcingle, if used according to the instructions given for acquiring a seat, will make a better rider of you because it will teach you to ride on a balance, not grip, and will get you away from the idea of depending on the cantle and fork to keep you on the horse. Not a great amount of credit is due anyone who depends on a fork and cantle and a death grip on the halter rein to keep him on an ordinary bucking horse. If you can stay in an English saddle or with only a surcingle with stirrups, ride on a slack rein and fan with your hat, you may boast that you are a rider. It can be done and it is done. Early day range men did practically just that in their slick saddles and frowned upon a rider who rode his reins.

When the training period is over, go back to the stock saddle if you wish. It is a real pleasure to ride a low roper on a trained horse.

As has been mentioned before, it is against the principles of good riding for the seat of a stock saddle to be built up in front since it prevents the rider from getting forward over the center of gravity of the horse when there is action. Worse than that, it throws him back on the loins of the horse where

The correct seat. The rider should attempt to approximate this position in all movements. (The sketch was made from a photograph of an old time range hand.)

little weight should be carried. Such position of the rider is very tiring to the horse on a long day's ride. The seats of the saddles of early day range men *were not built up in front* and they rode "forward."

6. THE SURCINGLE.   A surcingle with a ring on each side and one under the belly of the horse is often convenient when breaking a green range colt but is not absolutely necessary. It is used when a running W is found necessary. If it is intended to ride with the surcingle and stirrups, the stirrups should by all means be so attached to the surcingle that they will trip and release in case the rider is thrown or the horse falls and a foot fails to come free from the stirrup. This arrangement is found, or should be found, in all English type saddles.

If a surcingle is not handy and a running W is needed, use the saddle for attaching the ropes of the W.

7. HALF-HOBBLES AND THE RUNNING W.   By half-hobble is meant merely a short strap with buckle and a ring sewed into one side. If it is lined with a piece of soft leather or sheepskin it is easier on the pastern where it is attached when used. Two of these are needed. If no surcingle with rings is available and the saddle used to complete the running W, a strap with ring attached should be placed on the cinch directly under the horse's belly.

To complete the W, about 15 to 18 feet of half-inch rope or cord is needed. If you are using the saddle instead of a surcingle, proceed as follows: Start on the off (right) side of the horse and tie one end of the rope to the horn or to the forward saddle strings. From there, go through the ring in the half-hobble which has been buckled around the right pastern. Next, go through the ring on the cinch under the belly of the horse; then through the ring in the half-hobble on the left pastern; then through the left stirrup. As may be readily seen, you have a W. It is also readily seen why it is called a running W.

If a surcingle is used the rope is attached to the rings on the sides and under the belly to form the W.

HALTER BREAKING

Needless to say, the younger a horse is when halter broken, the easier it is to do it. In colts under six months of age, it is a matter of 20 or 30 minutes if you exercise only a small amount of judgment. Proceed as follows: If the colt is gentle, adjust a halter on his head. If he is wild, put him in a small corral and in the manner best suited to conditions (use a chute if you have one, otherwise a lasso) get a loop around his neck and work it up next to the ears. Adjust a halter, if you wish, but he may be taught easily with the rope alone. Frighten him as little as possible. Whistle or sing to keep him thinking everything is going to be all right. Naturally, he will fight the rope or halter and even the gentle colt will usually throw himself a few times in the course of halter breaking. Never put a hitch around a colt's nose in order to halter break him.

Halter breaking the green horse. Never pull a steady pull on a horse whether mounted or working from the ground. Pull and slack. Stay slack when the horse is doing what you want.

When the first fight is over, step to one side and give a light pull and *slack immediately*. He will usually start to fight again. Have patience and when he quits, pull again, causing him to take one or two steps toward you; then *slack immediately*. If possible, step up and scratch him on the side of the neck or behind the withers. Keep repeating this performance until when you pull and slack he takes a step or two towards you. This usually requires a little hard work and sweat. However, soon when you pull and slack a time or two he will step towards you if you are pulling to the side. He does this in order to induce you to slack and relieve pressure on his neck. Pet him often. Even a wild range colt under six months will allow you to do so in twenty minutes. Keep talking low or whistling. When you can easily turn him around either way by pulling and slacking, step out in front and begin over. He will usually fight for a few minutes but soon gives in and will follow you around the corral on a slack rope if, when he stops, you pull and slack. If you pull a steady pull, this system will not work.

When using this method to halter-break a colt, at the end of about ten minutes with seemingly no results, it is customary to hear, if there is present an observer who "has been around horses all his life," the remark, "Put a hitch around his nose and drag him from the saddle horn." Pay no attention to this and after a while the colt will learn what you want and act accordingly.

Sometimes in headstrong colts it is necessary to more than pull and slack. You may have to give short jerks on the rope, being careful to slack after each jerk; however do not become cruel in your methods.

If a grown horse is to be halter broken, it is recommended that, after haltering or putting on the hackamore (in a chute, by lassoing the neck and manipulating, or by front-footing and throwing if such rough treatment is absolutely necessary) he be tied to a strong post or tree, or to a high, strong pole or board fence, and allowed to fight awhile. This is not recommended by many good range men as occasionally a wild horse will injure himself but it seldom happens, practically never in a farm-raised horse. Needless to say, the horse should be tied inside an enclosure. You can help him out by standing behind him (out of reach) and after he has hung back for a minute or so, tap him with a whip or switch. He jumps forward naturally which produces slack in the rope. This is the occasion when he may injure himself if he is tied to a low fence. By letting him repeat this process several times it is the matter of a couple of hours until he will stand on a slack rope, but will run backward and fight, if a wild horse, upon the slightest provocation.

When he will stand on a slack rope, untie him and use the process described for the halter breaking of young colts. The horse will follow you around the corral on a slack rope in 30 minutes after untying him and will always lead on a slack rope if a steady pull is not used in case he balks.

Many good range men object to the tying of a grown, wild range horse to anything solid. They prefer to use a big horse and work from the saddle horn and there is much reason in their argument. My objection is that it takes much longer to teach the horse to stand on a slack rope and it is much harder on the gentle saddle horse and on the man.

Another effective method for halter-breaking a horse is as follows: In the manner best suited to the occasion, place a halter or hackamore on the horse's head. Next, tie up a hind foot as detailed under the section on breaking wild colts. In the case of wild colts or horses, this is often not an easy matter and can best be done in a chute when the hackamore or halter is placed on the head; or, if it is necessary that the horse be front-footed and thrown, the foot rope may be adjusted before he is allowed to rise. It is not necessary that the foot be raised high; merely very far forward is sufficient.

When the foot has been secured and the horse has quieted down, step to one side and begin to pull and slack on the lead rope or strap. Keep it up until, when you pull, he turns toward you readily from either side, pivoting on the free hind foot. Then remove the foot rope and work from in front. There will usually be a fight at first but, with some patience and continual pulling and slacking, in a short time the horse will follow you around the corral on a slack line.

Always in doing anything to an especially nervous or wild horse, much singing, talking, and whistling, and many unnecessary movements are very much indicated. However, seldom or never look the horse directly in the eye. He soon decides that he is not going to be hurt and becomes gentle much quicker than if handled as if he were a piece of fine china. At the same time, great care should be taken not to hit the horse unnecessarily nor do anything else to make him fear ordinary sensible treatment. If he "throws a fit" occasionally because you suddenly raise your hand or pat him, let him keep it up until he learns better. However, if in the process, you allow him to knock you down or kick you, that is your fault and not that of the horse. Do not punish him.

After a colt or horse has been halter broken and will follow you around on a slack halter rein, he should be taught to "lead" from the side, you walking at his *Teaching a* shoulder. This is very simple and easy to do. *Horse to Walk* Take him to a round corral, preferably, or to *Beside You* a small enclosure of some kind. With you at his left side near the shoulder facing with the horse, take the bridle, hackamore, or halter reins in your right hand 8 inches from the jaw and push forward, trying to induce him to go ahead with you at his side. He will usually refuse and become excited. The corral fence prevents him from escaping to the right, so he usually starts running backward. Go backward with him as long as he wants to keep it up, then try again. He will hesitate. At this time, with the short quirt in your left hand, or with the hand, reach around behind you and tap him along the side. He will usually jump forward and care must be taken not to stop him suddenly with the reins. Move fast with him if necessary and soon he will slow down or stop. Keep repeating this procedure being careful to keep the reins slack at all times, and in ten minutes, he will move around the corral freely with you walking at his shoulder and no pressure at all on the reins. He is guided chiefly with your body against his shoulder. Repeat these instructions while going to the right around the corral, reversing the method as just described. This is the correct way to "lead" a horse. There is never any "hanging back."

BREAKING

Ordinarily the breaking of the barn or farm-raised colt is very simple. All that is needed is an understanding of horse nature, and plenty of patience, the necessary equipment such as hackamore, bridle, blanket and saddle, and a small enclosure or corral.

The Barn-raised Colt

Do not start to break a colt unless you have a small enclosure in which to work, preferably a round corral of about 33 feet in diameter. One a little larger or a little smaller will do but this is about the best size. Any small enclosure with a good fence will do if a round corral is not available. If you intend to put on a demonstration, by all means have a good place in which to work; otherwise, your demonstration is apt to "backfire" on you. Never allow anyone to persuade you to work in an enclosure surrounded by wire or by a poor fence of any kind. You will usually regret it if you do.

We will take it for granted that the colt is halter-broken. Of course, it is a good idea to begin when he is young and let him wear a snaffle bridle and a saddle for an hour at a time around the corral every now and then but it is not absolutely necessary. After you have become experienced, you will find it is really a waste of time.

Proceed as follows: Adjust the hackamore so that the bosal it at least 2 inches above the nostrils. See that there are not too many turns of the mecate, so that the fiador knot is well away from the jaw, and the bosal fits loosely. Use the mecate as a longe line (18 or 20 feet) and with the long driving whip start the colt in a circle to the left around you, making him keep at the end of the line. A little trouble will be experienced in getting him to start because he does not know what you want but do not rush him, and soon he will get the idea of circling. When he has circled 3 minutes, begin quietly by saying "Whoa!" Of course he has no idea what you mean. Begin to flick the line, gradually becoming a little more severe.

Soon he will stop and face you wondering what it is all about. Go to him (not the reverse) and pat him on the neck to let him know he has done the right thing. Start him up again in the same direction and repeat the process until you *know* that he has learned the meaning of "Whoa." Then start circling him in the other direction and continue, stopping him often. He will be just as hard to start to the right as he was to the left. When you are absolutely sure he knows what is wanted, require him to stop suddenly at command by flicking the line forcefully, thus causing the bosal to slap him lightly across the nose. Keep this up until when you command "Whoa," he stops immediately and "freezes." At this time begin to go over him with your hands and absolutely require him to stand in his tracks on a slack line. Pat and rub him all over, beginning easily so he will not fear you. Get a little more rough all the time. At intervals circle and stop him suddenly. After accustoming him to the hands, begin rubbing and fanning him with your hat, a saddle blanket, and finally with newspapers or slicker or rattle a sack of tin cans around and over him. All that is necessary is to remember not to scare the colt, but to work up gradually to the sack of cans to *prevent* fear. If he moves at any time, except when you are ready for him to do so, use the longe line sharply, so that the bosal strikes him lightly across the nose, slacking *immediately* each time. Every time he is stopped on command, go to him on a slack line. Never tighten unless it is necessary, then pull and slack; never a steady pull. In less than thirty minutes, the average barn-raised colt, even one that is inclined to be "snorty," will "freeze" when you say "Whoa," and allow you to *run* to him from either side, waving a newspaper or rattling a sack of tin cans.

While working the horse on the longe line, and especially if you intend to make a rope horse of him, teach him, when you say, "Whoa," to stop at the end of the line and remain there. If he starts toward you, keep repeating the same words, "Hold it, hold it," and keep flicking the line, at the same time. After he has stood still for a minute or so, command "Come here," and pull and slack on the line. Always

use the same command, and in the same tone of voice. Soon he
will hold when you tell him to do so, and will also come to you
when you command, "Come here." All these commands,
"Whoa," "Hold it," and "Come here," can be taught in an hour.

When the colt will absolutely stand under any and all
circumstances, get something on which to stand so that you
are somewhat above him and place it by his side. At first he
is suspicious but soon quiets down. Begin to reach across his
back and pat him from ears to tail. Work from both sides.
Then quietly lie on your belly across his withers and back
and let him become accustomed to your weight. Stay only a
second or two the first time. Absolutely require him to stand
on a slack line. When he will bear your weight without
excitement, throw your leg across him and lie straddle of
his back, remembering to keep the head down. Quiet colts
are often caused to buck by suddenly seeing a man's head
with hat on towering over them. Lie flat patting him all
the while and moving your feet over his hips and loins. Stay
only a few seconds the first time, and slide off on the opposite
side. Repeat, reversing the side for mounting. Stay longer
each time. Finally before sliding off, gradually raise the
head, keeping the hat on, slightly above the colt's neck. Slide
off. Each time raise higher until finally you are sitting up
patting him, moving the arms and the legs about with no
excitement from the colt. During this process, should he
become excited and move, sharply jerk and *slack* the longe
line, or the hackamore reins and command, "Whoa." If he
does not stop, do not try to stay too long. Slide off his back,
and give him a forceful jerk on the longe line, and make him
"freeze" on command. Keep coolly and calmly repeating until
he stands absolutely still, and allows you to sit on his back
and move your hat or a newspaper or other similar object.
Remember to stay slack at all times.

When the colt will quietly stand and allow you to do
anything you please, pick up the hackamore reins and get
him used to your handling them, requiring him to stand still.
Then squeeze him intermittently with your legs (do not kick
nor use the heel back towards the flank) just back of where

the cinch would be if he were saddled. If he does not move (remember he has no idea what you want) cluck quietly to him. If he still does not move, tap him lightly on the hips or shoulder with a small stick, or the short, stiff quirt *being sure to squeeze him each time he is tapped* so that he will learn to go forward by use of the legs alone. He will step forward. Allow him to take only two or three steps the first time and stop him by a slight jerk of the reins and a command, "Whoa." Pat him and let him know that he has done the right thing. Repeat this until he steps forward the instant your legs are closed and without the use of the quirt. Allow him to walk farther each time until he is moving freely around the corral. *Do not try to guide him.*

By this time, the colt will not object to the saddle being thrown on his back, first letting him smell and examine it. It is when the cinch is tightened that he may show fight. Therefore, be careful and move slowly using the longe line all the time in light intermittent jerks or pulls, but staying *slack*. With most colts you will have little or no trouble, but occasionally one will try to buck. If he does, try to hold the saddle with one hand and stop him with the other by using the line and repeating, "Whoa." If he happens to throw the saddle, give him a real lesson in "freezing" when you say "Whoa." Repeat until the cinch is tight enough to hold the saddle. Do not make the mistake of cinching a colt tight. There is no object in it, and it is very irritating to him.

When the saddle is in place, start him *slowly* around you on the longe line, requiring him to stop often. Go to him at first slowly, then faster and faster and move stirrups, wave a slicker, anything for commotion, requiring him to stand. You will have little or no trouble by this time and soon can pop stirrup leathers, or can do anything else you wish. Finally tie various articles to the saddle—cans, newspapers, anything to make a noise—and longe him again. By this time, he is not excited, and does not object to anything you do. If, at any time, he should begin to buck, use the line forcefully, more or less "banging" him across the nose with the bosal. He soon learns that you will tolerate none of that.

At this time adjust the bridle on his head with snaffle bit, first removing the reins; or this can even be done before starting the colt, letting him become accustomed to the bit in his mouth. Now, standing at his left shoulder, reach across the saddle with short quirt in right hand and pick up the hackamore rein. Take the left rein in the left hand. Cluck quietly to the colt to start him, or tap him lightly with the quirt in order to induce him to move forward. Walk around the corral with him in this position until he moves freely, then begin to practice reining him, being sure to *pull and slack* and pushing the opposite rein against his neck each time he is made to change directions with the direct rein. This teaches him neck-reining and he will neck-rein a little the first ride if you handle him right. The third ride he should neck-rein fairly well. Stop him often by pulling and slacking and commanding "Whoa." In ten minutes he will turn in either direction or will stop by the use of the reins.

By this time (45 minutes average) he is becoming weary and does not object to anything you do. With much unnecessary movement and talking, gradually raise yourself in the left stirrup requiring him to stand on *slack rein*. Repeat on the right side several times. Finally swing into the saddle and sit still for a minute or so, patting and talking. Dismount. Repeat from the opposite side. After a while take a turn or two with the mecate on the bosal to make it fit more snugly. Settle yourself in the saddle, pick up the hackamore reins and quietly squeeze him with your legs (not heels) where they hang in the stirrups—not back towards the flank. If he does not move forward, tap him lightly with the quirt until he does, squeezing him with the legs each time he is tapped. In five minutes he will learn that the squeeze means to go forward and no tap of the quirt is needed. Allow him to move only two or three steps. If he starts to run or buck, yank him hard, say "Whoa" and *slack*. Stop him (stay slack) and pat him. Require him to move several steps but without use of the reins. Finally let him move all about the corral and begin quietly to rein and stop him. Keep it up five minutes, no more, and the first lesson is over. Unsaddle, talk to him, pat him, give him a carrot or a handful of grain. (Something besides sugar should be used to reward a horse. One that is continually fed any kind of tidbit is a nuisance.) With the average barn-raised colt, this lesson has lasted about one hour depending upon the nature of the individual colt and upon the proficiency of the trainer.

Next day adjust hackamore and bridle, and take him back to the small enclosure. Work on the longe line five minutes, requiring him to "freeze" often. Make him stand absolutely for saddling on *slack rein.* Do not be quiet. Talk, sing, wave the saddle blanket or hat, but never let anything strike the colt unnecessarily to scare him. Tie the sack of cans to the saddle, newspapers, anything to rattle. Start him on the longe line. If he tries to buck, use the longe line with force to teach him to attend to business—your business. When he has quieted and does not object to anything, mount slowly, awkwardly, always on a slack rein, requiring him absolutely to stand still until you squeeze him with the legs. Dismount. Mount in the same manner from the right side. Squeeze him with the legs and ride him around the corral fifteen or twenty minutes, reining according to the instructions already given and stopping often. Do much unnecessary moving of hands. Remove and wave your hat (always on slack rein). Act as if such antics are necessary and a part of the game. Any time he becomes excited, stop him abruptly with a jerk and slack and the command, "Whoa." *Repeat, repeat, repeat,* until the colt is not afraid of anything and you can rein and stop him at will in the small corral. Then ride into a larger corral or into the open for a period of ten minutes, and the second lesson is finished. Do not continue until the colt is tired.

Repeat the performance detailed above each day until he is absolutely unafraid and stops easily. The work on the longe line will be of shorter duration each day. With the average barn-raised colt that is nervous and "snorty," it is necessary to longe only about four or five days for five minutes each day before mounting; the gentle kind about twice. Now and then, there is found a colt of odd nature. He must be dealt with according to that nature, the breaker using good judgment. For breaking the kind that every now and then "grab" themselves, "swallow their tails" and start running and bucking, see the instructions for breaking wild colts.

It is not intended that this course should start amateurs and inexperienced horse lovers working with wild colts as *Breaking the Wild Range Colt* only experienced hands know how easy it is to be seriously injured. If you are an amateur, wait until you have been around and *assisted* with such horses for a year or more before trying this method out for yourself.

In the correct and easy breaking of wild range colts remember that the main thing is to teach the *horse* not to be afraid of *you*. If you think seriously, you will admit that you are afraid of him because you know that he can kill you if he gains the advantage. The fact that he puts up a fight should not be held against him. It is *not* meanness. He thinks you are going to abuse or injure him. It is nature's law of self-preservation. It is your place to show him very quickly that no harm will come to him. This can be done with the average wild colt in about thirty minutes from the time you lead him into the round corral. From there on out the breaking is a matter of routine.

Range colts should be broken before they are four years old if possible; before they develop too much willpower of their own. If it is possible to do so, the bunch should be brought into the corrals and fed hay a few days to allow them to become accustomed to the life about the ranch. It is a good idea to go among them often, talking quietly, singing or whistling at first; later purposely creating a commotion and without looking directly at the colts, act as if things like that go on all the time and do not amount to anything. If this has been done when they are yearlings or twos, they are already prepared. It is taken for granted at this time that they are already halter broken according to instructions on that subject. That being the case, proceed with each colt as follows:

Run the horse into the round corral. Catch him by talking and easy manipulation if possible. If not, use a chute. If there is no chute, quietly rope him. Adjust the hackamore so that the bosal is high above the nostrils and very loose—never low. After a little getting acquainted, take about twenty feet of ¾″ rope and tie a loop that will not draw tight snugly at one end around the horse's neck just in front of the shoulders. Double the rope back through this loop to make another loop long enough to reach the hind foot. Spread this loop on the ground under the horse and lead him forward a step so that he steps in it with either hind foot. Now is the time to be quick and careful and is the only time in the process of breaking that the colt need have fear and think you intend to do him harm. It is regrettable that such is the case, but it is necessary. The next step is much easier if you have an assistant to handle either the hackamore lead rope or the foot rope; but if you are alone proceed as follows: Take a fairly short hold on the lead rope with one hand (use judgment) and as short as possible on the foot rope with the other. Then with the hand in which the lead rope is held also catch the foot rope, thus using both hands upon the latter. With a quick jerk take the hind foot off the ground (the foot rope is under the pastern) and set back and hold ropes. Naturally there is a fight, the seriousness of which depends upon the individual horse. If you manipulate correctly you will keep the foot off the ground and at the same time cause the fight to progress in short circles. Be sure to have everything right before you start, so that you do not allow any slipping of the foot rope. If you do allow it to slip, there will be a rope burn. With a little practice, you will become adept at this and will not burn one colt in ten and that one only to a slight degree. When the fight is over, pull the foot up high and tie securely to the loop around the base of the neck. The colt is now at your mercy so act accordingly, and let him know that you regret having had to go through with such maneuvers. Sometimes the securing of the hind foot is not easy, and may take some time and much maneuvering. *Have patience. Do not lose your temper. Do not blame the colt.*

After a short breathing spell, begin rubbing (not slapping) the horse with your hands. Start at his forehead (Keep hands off a colt's nose.) and cover every square inch of his body right down to each hoof. Go easy at first, keeping up an incessant line of talking or singing or whistling. Gradually become more rough as he loses his fear and keep on until you can pat him recklessly all over. Then take your hat or a gunny-sack, let him smell and examine it, and begin to rub him with that, being sure to include all the legs. As he loses fear, work faster and rougher (use judgment) and soon he does not care what you do. From the gunny-sack, change to a large saddle blanket, then to a slicker, then to a newspaper, and finally to a sack of tin cans, taking care all the time not to work too fast and rough, and every now and then letting his foot down and changing the rope to the opposite foot. In thirty minutes it is possible to easily teach the ordinary wild colt that no harm will come to him, and you may do anything you like around him without the foot rope.

Teaching the colt not to be afraid of you. This is much more important than it is for you not to be afraid of him.

Next, again tie up a foot, and get something on which to stand eighteen to twenty-four inches in height. Place this beside the colt and mount the object. This will produce at least suspicion at first. When he is over that, lean over him and begin to pat the opposite side from ears to tail, talking all the while. Next, put some weight across his withers and back, lying on belly, and continue patting. Do not stay but a few seconds. Repeat, staying longer. Soon you can bear your whole weight across him, without a fight. Repeat this entire performance on the opposite side. When he makes no objection whatever, quietly lie on his back lengthwise, *keeping your head down* and talking and patting and moving the feet. Stay but a few seconds at first, then longer until he pays no attention. Finally lie on his back, and begin to raise the head, hat on; keep talking and patting. Soon you can sit up and wave the arms, move the legs and rattle a sack of cans. If at any time there is a fight, stay with it and keep repeating until you win. If he happens to get you off, it is not serious if you finally win. Now, dismount, let the foot down and allow him to rest. After a few minutes start him circling around you on the longe line (lead rope) and teach him to "freeze" at the command "Whoa" according to the instructions given in the section on breaking the farm-raised colt. Be no rougher than is necessary, but make many unnecessary movements and much commotion—sing, whistle, talk. When he will absolutely "freeze" at the word, "Whoa," tie up a hind foot again. Bring out the saddle and blanket and *let him smell and examine them.* Adjust a snaffle bridle without reins on his head. Roughly throw the blanket on his back, then the saddle, being careful not to allow the off stirrup or the cinch to hurt his leg on the off side. *Do everything on a slack line or rein.* If he moves, jerk sharply on the line and *slack immediately.* Bounce the saddle up and down on his back; slide it up to his ears and back on his rump. When he no longer pays attention, settle it in place and cinch just barely snug. If he objects to the cinch, which is often the case, do some manipulating until he ceases to object. Wait a minute and tighten the cinch until you know he cannot throw the saddle, but not as tight as you can get it. This is very important. *Tight cinches have ruined more horses than almost any one thing.*

Let the foot down and allow him to stand a minute or two, talking all the while. Then get ready for action and

start him circling. If he starts bucking, set him down sharply
with the longe line and start over. With fifteen feet of longe
line and the loose bosal, you can stop almost anything by
banging the bosal across his nose, causing the fiador knot to
strike under the lower jaw. Keep it up until he will go readily
in either direction without excitement. Stop him and tie
various articles on the saddle—canvas, slicker, newspapers,
cans. Start him easily, and soon he will not object to anything you do. Command "Whoa." Run to him on slack line;
bang stirrup leathers, shake slicker and papers, rattle cans
until he absolutely will stand on slack line. Rest.

Now, face with the colt. Take stiff quirt in right hand,
pass it across the saddle and pick up the right hackamore
rein. Take left rein in left hand. Cluck to the colt and push
him with your body and otherwise try to coax him to move
forward. If he does not understand, begin to tap lightly with
the quirt. Let him move a few steps, pull and slack on the
reins and command "Whoa." Repeat until he will stop by
manipulation of the reins alone. Next, teach him to turn

Work on the longe line. Teaching the green horse to listen to and
obey the trainer and not to fear articles tied to the saddle.

either way by use of the reins, by pulling and slacking on
the direct rein and pushing and slacking at the same time
on the indirect rein (the rein on the opposite side to which
you are going). At first, require only a step or two in the

direction indicated. Then four steps and finally, require him to turn half way around. Next, start him forward and rein him for a few minutes around the corral in figure 8's, stopping him every now and then by pulling and slacking. He is now ready for mounting. He has been taught *not to fear you, to stop when you pull and slack, and to rein in either direction.* The causes for his bucking or stampeding have been removed. This teaching the colt the use of the reins before mounting is very important and is very easy to do.

Adjust the foot rope again and take a hind foot, but do not pull it off the ground; only very far forward. Shake the saddle, pop stirrup leathers, rattle paper, slicker and cans. With lead rope in hand, but not tight, step in either stirrup and stand for a second. If he objects, jerk sharply with rope and command "Whoa." Repeat on the opposite side, and then many times on both sides. Keep getting nearer to the seat of the saddle. Finally, swing a leg across and sit quietly, talking and patting. He will usually not object, but if he does, jerk hard on the line and command "Whoa." Keep it up until he stands quietly. With a hind foot pulled forward and for the most part helpless, he will not fight long. When he has quieted, begin moving about in the saddle, slide over the cantle on his rump, wave the slicker around, rattle the sack of cans. He usually makes no objection at all by this time.

Dismount. Remove the foot rope but leave the slicker, paper and cans tied to the saddle. Take a turn or two with the mecate on the bosal in order to make it fit more snugly around his nose. Mount again from both sides, requiring him to stand. Finally, settle into the saddle, pick up the reins and quietly squeeze him with the legs (Do not kick) clucking quietly. If he refuses to move, tap his shoulders lightly with the quirt, squeezing at the same time with the legs. Allow him to move only a few steps the first time. There will seldom be any trouble, but if he becomes excited and acts as if he wants to buck, jerk sharply and *slack* and command, "Whoa." Keep it up until you are moving around the corral freely with no trouble and he starts when squeezed with the legs. Then begin to rein him in figure 8's, talking all the

while, and rattling the slicker and cans. Keep it up for ten
minutes, making him trot fast part of the time. Dismount.
The colt by now is very tired. The first lesson is finished.

A bet may be won on breaking a wild colt in two hours
by these methods so that he may be ridden slowly across
country alone, the rider waving an open newspaper or a
slicker, without any running or bucking. Occasionally you
will lose this bet but you will win eight times out of ten.

A bet may also be won on a horse that has previously
been broken and is hard to mount, that you can mount him
from either side in thirty minutes and leave the reins on the
ground, using the longe line as hereinbefore detailed.

The next day when you first begin, the colt will be as
wild as ever and also somewhat sore. Go easy. Use judgment.
Longe him for a few minutes, stopping him often on command and moving a slicker or newspaper around him always
on a slack line. Saddle, requiring him to stand. You may
have some trouble. Tie a slicker, cans, or paper to the saddle.
Longe him five minutes, stopping often on command. Mount
on a slack rein. If he objects, you may have to pull a hind
foot forward with a foot rope. Repeat until all fear is gone.
Ride in the round corral for fifteen minutes at walk and
trot, mounting and dismounting often and rattling the things
tied on the saddle. When he reins and stops well and moves
forward when squeezed with the legs, open the gate and ride
into a larger corral. As yet he should not be ridden in the open.
Ride in the larger corral fifteen minutes, making him *gallop*
around once or twice. Dismount and unsaddle.

Repeat this performance each day until it is not necessary
to longe him at all before mounting and he reins well. After
the bridle-wising of the colt from the ground in the corral, he
may neck-rein a little at the end of his first ride if you use
the indirect rein strongly as well as the direct rein each time
you change directions. Use the indirect rein more and more
each ride, the direct rein less and less. (The direct rein is the
rein on the side to which you are reining; the indirect rein is
the rein on the opposite side.) Then ride into the open; make
him trot and gallop a little each day. Always carry slicker,

paper and cans and rattle them often. The colt is now broken and may be ridden anywhere alone. You may now cease tying things to the saddle as he does not care what you do. With the ordinary wild colt the training up to this point takes about a week or ten days; with some colts two weeks or more; but by now it is possible for a lady to ride them without any trouble. About the fourth or fifth ride is the time to be careful. The horse has been thinking and will usually try you out to see if you still are in command. Much judgment is needed at this time, more than for the first ride. It is easy for the breaker to win the argument using the method detailed and using ordinary horse-sense. Be firm when necessary and use the longe line forceably, but never be abusive, never lose your temper even if you are hurt.

There are many things to remember in this method of breaking wild colts. One is that *no colt is mean* even if he half kills you. He is scared. There are no mean horses anywhere, until some man makes them that way. Have patience. Use horse-sense. Do everything on a slack rein, especially mounting and dismounting. The chief reason for a horse becoming hard to mount is the fact that the rider mounts on a tight rein and jerks the horse's mouth or head when he swings into the saddle.

Now and then in breaking young horses, one is encountered that seems to be entirely different from all the others. He may be barn-raised or wild. He remains *Odd Horses—* "snorty" and ready to fight. He acts as if he *the Running W* could not stand the cinch. He tries to buck each day when first longed with the saddle, and then tries it with the rider. He refuses to believe that cans, slickers and papers will not injure him and continues to act accordingly. Many "grab" themselves often when mounted, let out a loud grunt or a bellow and suddenly start bucking. The actions seem almost involuntary. For the breaker of these horses, the sensible method is the running W. As has been explained under the equipment section, the running W is made with a half hobble for each front pastern, a short strap with ring attached to be buckled around the cinch under the horse's belly, and 15 to 18 feet of ½" rope or sash cord.

By the time it has been found out that a colt is of an odd or treacherous nature he has already been taught to stop suddenly at the command "Whoa" and has been worked over with newspapers, slickers and tin cans. Also, usually he may be saddled but will often throw the saddle before the cinch is tightened. In such cases, take the colt into the round corral and proceed as follows: Adjust hackamore and put on surcingle with ring on each side, or keep trying until he is saddled. It may be necessary to tie up a hind foot to accomplish this. Next adjust the W according to instructions given in the section on equipment. This can be done best while the hind foot is tied up. In the following instructions, it is taken for granted that you are using a saddle instead of a surcingle.

Do something or arrange something on the saddle to cause the colt to start bucking or running as soon as the foot rope is released and he is started up, such as drawing the cinch extra tight, especially the flank cinch of a double-rigged saddle, or by tying cans and newspapers on the saddle

The Running W.

so that they hang low. Take the longe line in the left hand
and the rope of the W in the right hand and get in the center
of corral. Start him going to the left around you and when
he starts running or bucking *gradually* take his front feet
with the W, causing him to stumble and finally rest on
his knees. Hold in that position for a minute, talking or
whistling all the while. Let him up and start over. Each
time he tries to buck or run, put him on his knees taking
care not to throw him suddenly on his nose. In a short time
you may easily keep him in line by merely pulling on the
rope enough to hinder the movement of his front legs. It is
seldom necessary to put him on his knees more than twice.
Much good judgment and horse-sense should be used with a
running W in order not to injure a colt by throwing him on
his nose, nor break his spirit and make him afraid to move.
When you absolutely have him subdued, tie a small loop for
the hand in the foot rope (W) so that it may be used from
the saddle and *mount on a slack rein.* Require him absolutely
to stand. Dismount and mount from the other side. Each
time he starts bucking or otherwise misbehaving, tighten the
W enough to make him straighten up. It will not be necessary
to throw him, and you need have no fear of riding with the W
if you have handled horses enough to be breaking out those of
this nature.

Proceed with the breaking the same as with any other
horse except to use the running W until the colt gives in and
stops trying to buck or run. He may be trotted or galloped
or even run with the W attached if the slack is kept out of
the rope. I have seen colts on which it was necessary to use
the running W every day for three weeks. Others give up
very quickly. All may be subdued with it. If used with judgment, it may be used in breaking all colts. It saves much
time and trouble in breaking any colt to drive (which does not
concern us here).

Horses that, for no apparent reason, start a habit of
bucking, those that become "barn-sour" and refuse to leave
headquarters, or those that play up too much, may be
straightened out in either of two ways: (1) the use of the

quirt or (2) the running W. Before deciding on the first method, be sure you understand what you are doing and that you can sit well enough to win; also make up your mind not to loose your temper, or you will spoil the horse. If it is a case of not wanting to leave the stable or of playing up too much, merely ride on a slack rein, use the legs strongly all the time, and when he whirls to the left, tap him lightly with the stiff quirt on the left side of the nose. This will surprise him and he will whirl in the other direction. Be ready for this and catch him on the right side of the nose as he whirls. *Keep using the legs strongly.* Continue this procedure and in a very short time he settles down and will go anywhere willingly.

If he starts the habit of bucking and seems to like it and you wish to take it out of him with the quirt, be extra sure you can ride. When he starts bucking, shake the reins out, give him his head and standing in the stirrups and riding forward use the quirt mercilessly across his shoulders and around his body until he quits. Then quietly talk to him and give him a pat. Invite him to start bucking again and repeat. Every time he bucks, do not try to hold him in, but give him his head and whip every jump. Never use spurs. In about two such lessons, he is usually "cured." However, if he throws you he is a spoiled horse, and resort must be had to the running W and it is possible now that it may fail.

If you choose the second method, the running W, first teach him its use according to the instructions previously given, so that you will not throw him when mounted, and proceed to ride him with it. Every time he starts one of his bad habits, lightly use the W so as to interfere with the action of his feet. He will remember his lessons in the corral and will straighten out and do whatever you require for fear of being thrown to his knees. This method takes longer but is the safer and more scientific of the two. It is often necessary to ride some horses that acquire a habit of bucking for a period of several weeks with the running W. "Barn-sour" horses (horses that do not want to leave the barn) may be changed with only a lesson or two.

Young horses, broken and handled according to the instructions given above, may be turned out for a year and ridden easily without trouble by first putting them on the longe line for five minutes, then saddling them more or less roughly (using judgment) then longeing them another five minutes requiring them to stop often on command and popping stirrup leathers and waving a slicker. After this, they may be mounted and ridden off about as when you finished breaking. If you do not go through with this procedure, you may start the horse to bucking.

This system of breaking and handling horses is not for those who believe in *forcing* horses to do their bidding instead of *teaching*. If you want to show the world that you are a "bronc twister" you have no need of these instructions anyway.

Do not expect to accomplish very much toward the breaking or training of your horse if you are able to give only one or two lessons per week instead of one every day. Young horses that are ridden only occasionally often seem to think up some kind of devilment in their idle hours. Especially is it important in the breaking of colts or young horses to give a lesson each day for two weeks; at the end of which period they are usually pretty well broken if handled right. When it is absolutely necessary to skip a few days in either breaking or training, the young horse should be longed for five or ten minutes before mounting. This work on the longe line is very important and can hardly be overdone.

In breaking, it is best to ride the young horse alone the first half dozen times at least. By starting him alone, he does not get the idea that another horse must accompany him before he can leave the stable or corral. The first time another horse is ridden with him, start the other horse in the lead, not behind the colt. After he is accustomed to the presence of the other horse, gradually bring the two side by side and later drop the other horse behind, thus gradually accustoming the colt to the idea that the whereabouts of the other horse does not matter. Especially is it important in the breaking of wild colts to ride the other horse in the lead. To them, the presence of a mounted horse behind them has always meant a chase and it is natural for them to want to run when the hazer comes out behind. (The hazer is the man who rides the broken horse out of the corral with the breaker on the green one.)

TRAINING

After the breaking process, if you are going to be a successful trainer, it is first necessary that you ride correctly. You must first have a good seat as discussed under the section on riding. You will not be successful if you ride the reins when a horse plays up, if you lose your balance when he whirls, if you do not above all things have or develop light hands—hands that merely feel the bit as you ride and slack completely when you stop; that never pull a steady pull on a horse's mouth but that work from a soft wrist with flexible fingers, whether you are on the ground leading a horse or on his back executing complicated maneuvers. It will do no good to demonstrate under pressure that you have light hands if they become heavy when you work.

A good seat is acquired by first learning and using the correct position in a saddle and then by much practice at all gaits and under unfavorable conditions, such as galloping down the side of a steep hill, over rocks, sagebrush and badger holes without interfering with the horse by riding the reins or gripping to any extent with the legs. If you assume the correct position, it is not necessary for you to grip.

If you are following these instructions and cannot seem to get results, it is because your seat is poor or your hands are heavy and incorrectly used, or you fail to constantly use the legs in every movement and also when just riding along; or you have no tact with a horse. In the latter case, it would be better if you learned to ride as best you can and let some-one else train your horse. However, no one can properly ride a trained horse who knows nothing about riding and horse-manship. It is a waste of time and money to have a horse trained and not take lessons yourself in riding him. It helps not one whit to tell the trainer of your horse that the horse is not trained and does not turn on his hind feet if the trainer tries you out and finds that if you wish to whirl to the left, you are using the *left* leg instead of the *right*, and have you lamely say, "Oh, I forgot," or "I did not understand it that way." It helps no more if you claim these instructions will not work to have you say the same things or similar when you do not obtain the desired results.

Learn to Ride. Think.

Any unbroken horse or any good healthy horse, when loose in a pasture, is supple and light and turns on his hind *Suppling a* feet, but becomes the opposite when broken and *Horse and* mounted. I do not know the reason. Most horses *Making Him* will even turn on their front feet when being led *Light* with only a halter on their heads. *Absolutely the chief object in training should be to produce suppleness and lightness first,* no matter what you wish the end results to be. The horse must be supple and light to properly stop and turn on hind feet, to perform special gaits properly, or to perform the many intricate movements of high school. Therefore, take great pains and much time in following these instructions.

The horse has been broken. By that is meant he has lost his fear, has lost any tendency to run or buck. He should be neck-reining well by this time if properly ridden. He will move forward promptly when the legs are closed against his side. He checks or stops when the reins are fingered and the body leaned slightly backward. He is now ready for more intensive training.

So far he has been ridden with a hackamore but carrying a snaffle bridle without reins. **Horses that have been broken and ridden for some time by incorrect methods respond to the same training as do colts broken according to the methods described in the section on breaking. It merely takes longer, usually much longer. These horses should first be worked on the longe line and taught to "freeze" on the command, "Whoa." Then proceed the same as with colts broken according to the methods herein detailed.**

Attach light reins (never heavy reins) to the snaffle bit. Begin riding the colt on the hackamore but fingering the bridle reins more than is necessary. When you stop or turn, be sure that half the pressure is on the bridle reins. Start teaching him to extend himself and walk fast. Do this by constant use of the legs, squeezing at about every other step and lightly fingering the reins to check him if he breaks into a dog-trot. Use the legs where they hang in the stirrups, not back towards the flank. *Do not kick.* The pressure should be exerted from the ankles to the thighs but chiefly in the calves. Try to feel it and check him *before* he breaks into the trot. Squeeze immediately. If he tries to trot again, check again. Each time you check, immediately squeeze and slack off on the reins. Keep this up, the alternate use of hands and legs, and in a few lessons of one hour each, you will see good results. Any horse may be taught a fast walk.

It is hard for an amateur trainer to realize when starting a quiet, gentle colt that pays little or no attention at first to the use of the legs that, in time, if handled correctly, he will not allow himself to be squeezed in the least with the calves without immediately going into action; or, if one leg only is used, immediately moving his hind quarters in the opposite direction. To speed up this immediate response, it is better to use light taps of the quirt as the horse is squeezed than it is to kick him in the flank with the heels—the usual method.

Rein and change directions often, using the indirect rein more all the time (neck rein). At first change directions only slightly but as improvement is seen, rein at a more acute angle until he will turn easily at a 90 degree angle. Use the legs constantly. No matter what you wish to do, squeeze first to prepare the horse, then proceed with the movement. Now, if you rein to the *right*, use the *left leg* against the horse; if you rein to the *left*, use the *right leg*. Long before the horse is trained, he will rein on the legs alone and especially if you lean the body very slightly each time in the direction in which you are reining. It is not an easy matter for an amateur to learn to lean his body automatically one way and use the opposite leg. It is the tendency at first to use the leg on the side to which you are leaning.

During these first lessons in walking and getting used to the bit, push the horse into a free trot every now and then, but under no circumstances allow him to jog. Gradually push the trot until he is doing his best after a dozen lessons. It is all right to finish a lesson with a short free gallop, or even a run, so that the horse will not get the idea that he is never supposed to gallop with a rider on his back. *At all times use a light hand on the reins pulling and slacking imperceptibly from a soft wrist and with flexible fingers.* Keep crowding the horse in a walk until he is doing a slow fox-trot which is a half walk, half trot, but is definitely not a slow trot.

Up to this time, about two weeks in the case of the average horse properly broken in the hands of an experienced trainer, much longer in the case of an amateur and especially if his horse has been broken incorrectly, the horse has been traveling in an extended manner. That is, his hind feet are back, not under his body, his head and neck are low (the degree depending on the individual horse) his muzzle forward. It is now time to dispense with the hackamore and to teach him suppleness and collection.

After the horse is trained, he is allowed to extend himself on long rides, but when there is work to do or action wanted, it is absolutely necessary that he be collected. Collection is the gathering of the horse into one compact mass which almost acts as a unit. When collected, a horse's head is up, his nose is down (forehead perpendicular or almost), *his lower jaw relaxed and soft under light hands*, his hind feet well under the body. He is balanced and ready for any action or maneuver. A horse balances himself, when loose or when ridden, by raising and lowering his head and neck and by changing the relative position of his hind feet. The lower the head, the farther the hind feet must be pushed under the body for efficient balance. It is a mistaken idea that the head of a cow horse should be low when he works. Of course, it can be too high, up in the rider's face, but in any case, it should be above the level. It interferes with nothing here, usual opinion to the contrary notwithstanding. With the head up, excessive effort is not necessary on the part of the horse, to bring the hind feet far enough forward to secure proper balance.

Setting of the horse's head, so that he carries it when

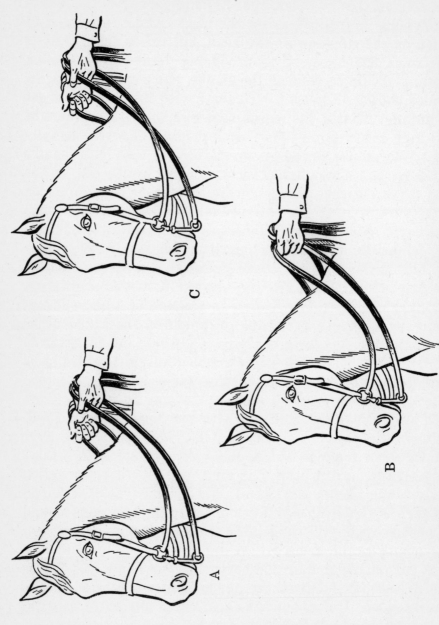

A. Correct Method of Holding reins of a Weymouth or Pelham bridle for efficient use in training.
B. Correct Method of Using Reins of a Weymouth or Pelham bridle with one hand.
C. Incorrect and Inefficient method of using reins of Weymouth or Pelham Bridle. Such method defeats the purpose for which two bits is intended.

ridden in any desired position, is done by light hands acting properly on the bit. Continual light fingering of the snaffle as the horse is trained, raises the head. Almost any kind of action on the curb lowers the head, but raises the muzzle if the hands are heavy, thus producing "star-gazers." Most training should be done on the snaffle, but experienced light-handed trainers can use a curb along with the snaffle to great advantage. That is the reason that fine trainers, trainers of real high school horses (not trick or circus horses) usually use a Weymouth bridle—a double bridle with both snaffle and curb, but some of the best use only a snaffle bit. It has been my experience that very few horsemen have any idea of the purpose of the two bits, snaffle and curb, in the mouth of a horse. Many explanations may be heard, some of them very amusing, such as the idea that you ride a horse with two bits so that you can *hold* him; or that a horse performs one gait better on one bit, and another better on a different bit. Such could possibly be true in the case of a horse *forced* to do certain gaits by means of weighted shoes and other mechanical devices, by a heavy-handed rider, but is certainly not true of a horse first made supple and light before he is gaited. Only a trainer has any use for a Weymouth bridle. After a horse is *properly* trained, he may be easily ridden with either curb or snaffle or with the hackamore and will perform the same on either, but the rider must have light hands. Since the idea of a double bridle (Weymouth bridle) is to set the horse's head, and since a light fingering action on the snaffle bit raises the head and the same type of action on the curb lowers it, it is self evident that the two reins should be held accordingly, the snaffle above, the curb below, if a Weymouth bridle is used. Do not cross the reins and ride with curb above and snaffle below in your hand. As can be readily seen, this defeats the purpose for which the two bits was intended. Unless you are experienced and *know* that you have light hands, it is best to do your training with one bit only, the snaffle. Later, when the horse is well along in training, the change may be made to the curb, and the horse will not object *if you use light hands.*

Anyone capable of properly using a severe bit of any type needs no such instrument for riding a horse. Others, in my opinion, should not be allowed to use one. Use only a snaffle or bar and a simple curb with low port.

So much for bits.

In order to teach a horse collection, begin using the legs strongly, which causes him to push his hind feet farther under his body and to start moving forward faster.

Collection At the same time, begin using the hands lightly on the bit, exercising much judgment as to how strongly to use them, in order to cause the horse to gradually raise the head and flex his neck at the poll (just back of the head), not at the withers (which would of necessity produce a low head). Keep up this simple process, constant and intermittent use of hands and legs until the horse at an instant's indication will gather himself with hind feet well under body, head slightly up, nose *down*, forehead almost perpendicular. If you have used light hands, by this time he will be traveling and performing with *lower jaw relaxed and soft* against the bit. Sometimes it helps materially to give lessons from the ground in flexing the neck at the poll when the reins are fingered. This is done as follows: Stand at the left shoulder facing in the same direction as the horse, reins across horse's neck or the saddle. Hold to saddle with the right hand to steady yourself. Grasp both reins in left hand about six inches from the bit. Begin working the hands lightly backward and slightly upward (to raise the horse's head) using fast intermittent pulling and slacking (a tremor) in order to induce the horse to flex his neck at the poll. At first this usually has the opposite effect and the horse "shoots" the muzzle forward. Do not fight this movement, but *give* when he *takes*, and immediately begin over. Soon you will feel the muscles of his neck and jaw relax and his muzzle will be brought "in" toward his chest. *Slack immediately* and let him know he has pleased you. Wait a few seconds and repeat. Never keep up any procedure on a horse in training until he is tired of it—"soured." In a lesson or two, he will "give" his mouth to you at only a slight action from your hand. By using the same procedure when mounted, the horse is soon *traveling forward* with chin "in" and *lower jaw relaxed*, when the legs are used sufficiently to keep him on the bit. When this is the case, the hind feet will also be well under the body. *It is absolutely necessary that he travel and perform with soft, relaxed lower jaw.* A mere "tucking in" of the chin and muzzle is not sufficient. A horse traveling with a hard, tense under-jaw and holding the bit tight in his mouth, cannot possibly be light, which is the case in so-called hard-mouthed horses. Only light hands

Collected and working on the haunches. This means that he has been taught to respond absolutely to hands and legs.

and constant use of the legs can produce the desired result, and it is not produced in a few lessons. *It requires many lessons, much patience, and hard work,* but the end result is worth any effort. After you have made one horse light, you will understand this method and will consider no other. *Producing lightness in a horse is the essence of fine horse training.* It is not easy to learn. When a horse is light he waits for and expects indications from his rider as to what is wanted. With slight use of the legs he goes into the bit but

Horse Traveling "Light." No pressure on the bit, hind feet well under body. If instructions in this book are followed, your horse will travel in this manner.

very lightly. With slight use of the hands he is back on the legs which should support him unless he is expected to back. Backing will be taken up later in these instructions. Here, it is well to repeat that an amateur when starting to train a quiet, gentle colt, can hardly realize that in from one to three months' training in the use of hands and legs, this same quiet colt that at first seemed to pay no attention at all to his efforts, will not allow any pressure whatever from the legs, no matter how slight, without going into action with his hind feet and will not bore into the bit at all against light hands. Such a horse, if both hands and legs are used properly, will stand and lightly "mark time" without excitement. If you are an amateur, however, do not expect to produce this effect on your first horse.

Training for lightness and collection is done chiefly at the walk; altogether at that gait to begin with, later moving at the trot. A good test for lightness and also an aid in training for it, is to suddenly rein often to right or left, and to check or stop often using the legs constantly, even when stopping. If the muzzle is pushed forward and the lower jaw is felt solidly against the bit, or if the head is thrown to one side with the same effect, *the horse is not light*. At first the reining should be done at only a slight angle, gradually increasing it until you are reining at an angle of ninety degrees and finally are whirling the horse completely around without any opposition whatever on the bit. Continue until he can be suddenly checked from a collected trot and whirled coolly, calmly and easily. *The horse is now collected and light and may be taught any gait or movement easily.*

The last word in lightness in a horse is seen in the real high school horse (not trick or circus horse). Such a horse is often booked for performances as a "dancing horse." The exhibition is really an exhibition of the rider and trainer but of course the crowd watches the horse and remarks that he is "very intelligent." Next time you have the opportunity, watch the rider instead and if you are unable to detect any signal whatever, you are witnessing a fine performance. If there is visible effort on the part of the rider, it means one of two things, viz.:

Horse Traveling "Heavy." Lower jaw rigid, and tight against the bit. Every movement indicating stiffness.

the horse is not finished or the trainer is lacking in ability. When your stock horse is trained according to these instructions, it will not be necessary for you to use visible effort in order to have him perform, such as raising the hands and swinging them right or left to make him rein fast, kicking him in the ribs or flanks to make him go forward, or using a strong and steady pull on the reins to have him slow or stop.

In all the training for suppleness and lightness, be sure to use the legs and body properly and constantly. Squeeze often. Use the left leg strongly when you rein to the right, and lean your body slightly to the right. Use the right leg strongly when you rein to the left, and lean your body slightly to the left. Use both legs when it is desired to go forward and also use both legs when stopping. Spoiled runaway horses and so-called hard-mouthed race horses may be made light over a period of time by using this method.

Making a horse supple and light is by far the most important part of training. It may require a long time, sometimes months, or you may see results very quickly. Do not begin training for anything except the walk, trot, and fox-trot until you are sure the horse is supple and light.

A horse that refuses to go into the bit, but is behind it, is difficult if not impossible to control. He should be crowded into the bit by strong use of the legs. Rearing horses *Behind the Bit* are behind the bit. A horse crowded into the bit seldom or never rears. Much training and use of the legs is necessary in order to obtain quick response, and under all circumstances prevent a horse from getting behind the bit. A horse seldom rears with a good horseman, practically never, unless such an antic is desired and indicated. It is very easy to induce purposely a *light* horse to rear coolly and calmly and without danger.

While the lessons in lightness and flexion are in progress, lessons in advanced suppling should be given at the same time. Such lessons teach a horse to respond to *Advanced Suppling* hands and legs separately, the hands controlling the fore parts of the horse, the legs and hind parts. In fact, it is necessary that there be instant response from the use of hands and legs before lightness is attained. The reining test for lightness cannot be used successfully unless there is instant response to either leg used alone.

With reins over the horse's neck, stand at left shoulder facing the horse and take the left rein in left hand

A step in suppling. Rotating the horse on the forehand. Front feet
should remain stationary.

10 inches from the bit. Double the right hand into a fist and
with fist exert strong pressure in the side of the horse just
back of the cinch where the calf of the leg would be if you
were mounted. Induce the horse to move hind parts *only* in
the opposite direction. It is usually necessary to pull the head
slightly towards you with the rein at first in order to obtain
this result. At the first "give" of the hind parts, cease all
action immediately and let him know he has pleased you.
Repeat a few times, securing several side steps with the hind
parts. Reverse the process and repeat on the off side. Soon
he will move the hind parts either way when firm pressure
is applied with the fist and the rein is held lightly. Do not
prolong the process until the horse resents it. Next, and
during the same lesson, with the reins over the horse's neck,
face with the horse standing at left shoulder and take the
right rein in right hand and left rein in left hand. Use both
reins lightly to the side and slightly backwards to induce the
horse to move front quarters only to the left. This he will
consistently refuse to do at first and much manipulation and
patience is required. At the first step towards you, with front
feet only, cease action and give him a pat and a kind word.
Repeat, obtaining two or more steps. Reverse the process on
the off side.

A step in suppling. Teaching the use of the reins; rotating the horse on the haunches. Hind feet should remain stationary.

Before mounting each day, go through these exercises for a period of ten or fifteen minutes until in a few days the horse responds quickly and will rotate either front or hind quarters when requested without moving the opposite quarter. It is not objectionable if there is an up-and-down movement of the feet in the stationary quarters, during either exercise and during the rotation of the fore quarters on the hind, a backward step or two is a good indication as long as there is no side movement.

When the horse responds well in these exercises from the ground, begin practicing from the mounted position *Fast Reining* using the calves of the legs with heels well down to obtain rotation of the hind quarters and at the same time steadying the front quarters with the reins. In the rotation of the front quarters to the *left*, the *right* leg should be used strongly and vice versa. The leg holds the hind quarters while the front rotates. Use the indirect rein more and more, the direct rein less and less. Keep requiring quicker response to hands and legs and greater speed in rotation. If the body is used to assist the aids (hands and legs), response is increased notably. For instance, when rotating the forequarters to the left, it is easy to see that most of the weight of the horse is on the left hind foot. So lean your body slightly to the left and slightly backward.

If the hind quarters are being rotated to the right, most of the weight is on the right fore leg, lean your body slightly forward and to the right. These rotation exercises if properly carried out, using much patience and good judgment, produce fast reining, and in one month's time the average horse may be spun on his hind feet in either direction. He will rein better at that time than the average horse that has worked cattle constantly for a year or more. However, you must be a good rider, not a rough rider. You must absolutely coordinate the use of hands, legs and body and practice diagonal horsemanship; that is, if you rein to the left use the right leg and lean the body slightly to the left; if you rein right, use the left leg and lean the body slightly to the right. In two months, the horse will rein well and fast on legs alone (no rein) if the body is used to assist.

Remember, these exercises are the key to fast reining, although one can hardly realize it. Just as soon as the horse will perform the rotation maneuvers well while mounted, he will surprise you at how fast he will rein while moving forward or when working stock. Naturally, the more adept he becomes at these maneuvers, the faster he will rein while in actual use.

When the horse will freely and easily perform the rotation maneuvers as described above, he may be readily taught to side-step. To side-step to the right, use the left **The** leg strongly to start the hind parts moving to the **Side-pass** right. Finger the reins lightly to prevent him from going forward, and at the same time push his front quarters to the right with the indirect (left) rein. Obtain two or three side steps and rest. Repeat. Using the opposite aids, cause him to side-step to the left. By going slowly and not overdoing it at any one time, the horse will do a side pass in a trot in a short time. In teaching the side pass, it is important to remember to lean the body slightly in the direction in which you are traveling. It is the tendency for an amateur to lean in the opposite direction. It is also the tendency to relax the leg when the reins are used. Needless to say, this allows the hind parts to get behind or stop.

If you are an amateur, do not think that all this is going to be easy. If you do not have patience and persistence, it is better not to start. If you are not an amateur, you will have little trouble.

When the horse will do the side-pass easily, and back (see instructions for backing) gates may be opened, entered, and shut from his back without dismounting.

Many horses become "sour" when training from so much use of the legs, in which case it is best to ride them a day or two and allow them to extend themselves and forget training; or to skip a few days entirely. Such horses back their ears and often kick when the legs are used to any extent. They will soon forget it if handled right.

When the horse will do the side-pass at the trot, it is a simple matter to teach him the serpentine at both trot and walk. First teach it at the walk. Keep the horse *The Serpentine* moving forward and by use of the hands and legs as detailed, cause him to keep his body straight and move several steps to one side while walking. Then, using the opposite aids move him back the same distance in the same manner, still going forward. At first require only two changes; later, any number. Continue until he will do the exercise easily at the trot. The serpentine amounts to little if a definite number of steps in each direction is not decided upon in advance. If you decide upon six steps, the aids (hands, legs, body) must be changed on the fifth.

When the horse has been trained thus far in suppleness and lightness, it is easy to be seen how he can be made to *Drunk Man* imitate a drunk person. Start him walking slowly moving two steps to the right, two steps forward, two or three steps to the left, using hands, legs and body so that it is not noticeable to an observer. Keep walking all the time, moving front quarters only to the right, forward a step or two, front quarters back, then hind quarters over, back the horse on the legs two steps (see instructions for backing) and so on. This makes an interesting demonstration.

The serpentine and the drunk man act should not be taught nor practiced until the horse has been finished in the walk, trot, canter and change of leads. Too much training and too fast will cause him to resent the aids. These two movements are merely stunts anyway and in no way enhance the future use of the horse. They merely show that he responds well to hands and legs.

Lateral Flexions and Suppleness of the Horse's Body This part of training is rather advanced and complicated and should not be attempted until you have learned to ride correctly according to the instructions set forth herein and have trained a horse or two. In fact, it is not too important because if your horse is trained otherwise properly and ridden correctly over a period of time, he will acquire the suppleness of body while mounted that is natural to him when free. After you are experienced, however, you can hasten the process by teaching the lateral flexions.

The idea in teaching the lateral flexions is to have the horse turn, and otherwise perform, with body muscles relaxed except for those necessarily used in executing the turn or maneuver. A light, well-suppled horse turns on hind feet as does the natural cutting horse, with body bent in the form of an arc, as does a trout turn on his tail in a tank of water and not as a log turns in a pond in one stiff, unbending mass or as a horse turns that has been made to turn with heavy hands on a severe bit, the roof of his mouth being gouged perhaps, or, at least, threatened and a bat or an electrically-charged rein being applied along his neck. Close observation of a good cutting horse in action and in the middle of a quick turn will disclose the fact that his body is not straight but is in the shape of an arc. The turn is done in the flash of an eye but for his body to assume this form his head had to start the turn, his neck follow, and so on down his body to his hind quarters which remain anchored in one spot until the turn is completed. Naturally, if a horse turns in this manner, his body cannot remain rigid as the log in the pond; as the horse that turns from fear. A more or less mechanical way of helping a horse to learn to bend his body on a turn after he has learned to respond to hands and legs is to ride him in a square or rectangular enclosure surrounded by a fence or wall and push him into each corner so closely that he is forced to turn his head first, then follow with his neck and body. If he tries to cut across the corner with his hind parts, and he usually does, it is then necessary to use the leg on the side to which he is turning and use it far back on his side to *hold* the hind parts to the wall. As aforesaid, this is mechanics and not good horsemanship. The rider depends on the wall and the corner to obtain the desired results and must use the leg and rein on the same side at the same time while good horsemanship demands that diagonal aids be used simultaneously; that is, left leg, right rein; right leg, left rein.

Other than good riding methods over a period of time, the scientific way to teach the mounted horse to relax and bend his body while turning, and the one in which good horsemanship must be used, is to teach the lateral flexions. After the horse has been suppled and made light and taught to respond to hands and legs according to previous instructions, this is done in the following manner: Mount the horse and by the use of hands and legs obtain collection and relaxation of the muscles of the lower jaw, head up. With a delicate fingering of one snaffle rein, induce the horse to turn head only at the poll at a slight angle, keeping the jaw relaxed. Reward with a pat and do the same on the opposite side. Continue the exercises a short time, then let him walk about as he pleases. Repeat this performance a half dozen times, then go about other things. At each lesson, require him to turn his head farther until, in a half dozen lessons he is turning it at right angles to his body, neck bent at the poll, not at the base. At this point, attempt to push him forward with the legs, keeping his head turned at right angles and *his jaw light against the bit*. You will always meet with resistance as it is natural for him to want to face in the direction in which he is advancing, but with perseverance, he will soon move a step or two forward. At this time, if the flexion is to the right, strongly use left leg six inches behind the cinch to prevent the horse from throwing haunches to the left and turning. Require only a step or two and reward. Obtain the flexion to the left in the same manner, reversing the process, of course. In the course of a few lessons, he will be traveling forward in a straight line with head turned at right angles either to right or left, collected and with lower jaw relaxed. With continued practice and stronger use of the leg, you may finally push his hindquarters slightly beyond the straight line on which he is walking, thus causing him to travel forward, body in the shape of an arc, front feet following the line, head and haunches bent slightly to the same side. Needless to say, when your horse is suppled to this extent by the correct use of hands and legs, you may cause him to perform almost any maneuver you may desire and when making a fast turn he will turn freely and easily with body "bent," as a horse turns naturally in a pasture or as a "natural-born cutting horse" turns with a rider on his back.

Cutting small figure 8's at walk, trot, and canter is a valuable means of keeping a well suppled horse in practice, using the legs and reins to see that he cuts them correctly, bending the body in an arc at the end of each 8; the outside leg strongly six inches behind the cinch, the inside leg at the cinch or in front of it. Both legs, of course, continue to push the horse forward.

Most good horses do a good trot almost from the beginning. If you push the horse in an extended trot while being broken, it is no trouble to have him do a collected trot **The Trot** in training while being made light. Merely put him into an extended trot and begin to finger the reins to check extended movement and at the same time use the legs enough to keep him lightly on the bit. In a very short time, he will do a collected trot and from there can be made to do a high trot which has no place in the work of a stock horse, but is very showy in a parade. To produce a high trot, use the legs more and more and even assist with light taps of the quirt to produce great animation, at the same time fingering the reins to prevent fast forward movement. The resulting energy which would be used to go forward will be used to raise the legs in a high trot.

In an extended trot, some horses have a tendency to reach farther on one diagonal than on the other. This tendency disappears when the collected trot is obtained. (The trot is a diagonal gait; that is, the horse moves one front and the opposite hind foot at the same time. The walk is also diagonal.)

The horse is now ready to be taught a slow three-beat canter and to change leads in the canter at the will of the rider; later to change of his own accord while gal-*The* loping or running each time there is a change of *Canter* direction to any extent.

The canter is a refined gallop, worked down by hands and legs until three distinct beats can be heard when working on firm ground. In a fast gallop all four feet are off the ground in each stride and they strike so near together that the beats blend, but when worked down to a slow canter, the feet strike so as to produce a definite 1-2-3, 1-2-3, 1-2-3. If the horse is leading with the legs on the off side (in a gallop or canter a horse leads with the two legs on one side or the other) the left fore strikes the ground first for beat one, the right fore and left hind strike in unison for beat two, and the right hind strikes for beat three. If a horse starts a gallop or canter or makes a flying change of leads incorrectly leading with either front and the opposite hind, it produces a violent rolling motion of his body which is very annoying to the rider and very dangerous for the horse if he is put into a run or worked on fast reining. He is apt to grab a front leg with a hind foot and throw himself or even break a leg. The properly suppled and collected horse seldom does this. He changes the hind feet first. The stiff-moving, poorly trained, extended horse often changes in front without changing behind.

When a horse goes into a canter or gallop, he first raises his entire front quarters and at almost the same instant

When a horse has advanced far enough in suppling, he may be stood
on hind feet without excitement and, by proper use of the rider's legs,
be caused to raise either foot as called for and stand for a second on
one hind foot.

uses powerful propulsion from his hind quarters, most of the
latter coming from the hind leg on the opposite side to which
he intends to lead. If he starts the lead with the left fore
and left hind, the strongest effort of propulsion will come
from his right hind leg and it will carry most of his weight
for an instant. All in the same movement his muzzle will be
tilted slightly up and to the left. To start teaching the canter,
it is best to begin by teaching the general signal or set of
signals for the canter paying no attention to leads and allow-
ing him to lead as he chooses. By this time he is responding
fairly well to the use of hands and legs and it is not difficult.
Proceed on the straightaway. Start the horse at the walk,
strongly using the legs, lift the reins definitely (the snaffle
rein if using the Weymouth bridle) and slack. At first he will
not know what is wanted, and will go into a fast trot. Keep
lifting and slacking on the reins and using the legs and by
repetition and urging with light taps of a stiff quirt, he will
soon get the idea and go into a fast gallop. By lightly using
the hands, slow him. He will then usually want to come back

to a trot at which time the legs must be strongly used. By keeping up this procedure, alternate use of hands and legs, in a few lessons he is doing a fairly slow canter. During this time he should be slowed often to a walk and started over in order to teach him the signal for going into the canter; namely, the closing of the legs and the lifting and slacking of the reins. Always start from the walk, but at first he will often go into a trot before getting into the stride of the gallop. It is not long, however, before he goes directly from the walk to the gallop or canter.

When he has learned the signal well and has begun to canter fairly slowly, it is time to think of putting him into either lead desired. Most horses are lefthanded. *Change of Leads* They prefer to canter on the left lead and, mounted, usually refuse to lead with the right foot, regardless of the fact that they do so when loose in the pasture. Any good horse is also very supple when playing in the pasture, but must be taught suppleness when mounted. The whole idea is to teach the horse to be as supple and as handy with his feet when mounted, as he is when turned loose.

In order to put the horse into a desired lead at the canter, he must first be put into a position which forces him to take this lead. If the right lead is desired, and his haunches are pushed slightly to the right with the left leg while walking, it is easily seen that the two feet on the right are then in the lead and must stay that way when given the canter signal unless the horse is allowed to take a quick step or two and throw himself out of position before going into the canter. This, some horses are very adept at doing, and they should be stopped and started over. Many horses become very excited and angry at this and much patience and tact is required in order to eventually obtain the desired results. If it seems almost impossible to obtain a right lead on the straightaway, it may be done by putting the horse into position and giving the signal on a turn to the right. Naturally, if circling to the right, a horse leads with two right feet; with the two left, if circling to the left. However, when mounted, most horses will not do this but will insist on cantering on one lead all the time, usually the left, until trained.

Before beginning the lessons in the leads, practice a few days at putting the haunches of the horse to either side while

Walking on Two Tracks

walking. This is called "walking on two tracks," the front feet making one track, the hind feet another. By this time it should not be necessary to explain that this is done by using the left leg to push haunches to the right and vice versa, steadying the front quarters at the same time with the hands to prevent a side pass. Practice until, when one leg is strongly used, the haunches are immediately felt to give and move over in the desired direction. This is the time to give the canter signal which he has already been taught to obey; that is, close both legs strongly and lift up and slack on the reins. There are two other ways to help at this time. First, using both hands on the reins when the legs are closed lean the body slightly backwards and to the *left* if a *right* lead is desired and carry both hands to the left. This lightens the entire right side of the horse and makes it easy and natural for him to take the right lead. If a left lead is desired, reverse the process. Lean the body slightly backward and to the right and carry the hands to the right. Second, when the reins are lifted, lift the right rein strong enough when a right lead is wanted, to tilt the muzzle of the horse slightly upward to the right, or to the left if a left lead is intended. It is easy to be seen that several indications must be made at almost the same instant, and much patience and practice is required in order to obtain good results. However, once these are obtained the amateur trainer may justly feel proud of himself. The next horse will be much easier. When the horse is trained to this degree, he will easily take either lead by merely lifting the rein on the side on which it is desired that he lead, and using the opposite leg.

There are two ways of determining on which side a horse is leading in a canter, when mounted, without leaning over and looking at the feet; a sign of an amateur. First, if he is leading with the two right feet, a glance downward at the point of his shoulder will show that the right side is about four inches in front of the left; a casual observance will also tell you that the horse's haunches are slightly to the right. Second, the leg of the rider, on the side on which the horse is leading, will be much in motion while the other leg will be comparatively still. If the horse is leading on the left side, the indications will of course be the opposite.

Now, the fundamental reason for teaching the horse to canter on either lead starting from a walk at the will of the rider, is to prepare him for changing in the air on a fast gallop or run whenever there is a change of direction, thus enabling him to brace himself properly on a turn and prevent a fall. This he does consistently when loose, but refuses to do so when mounted until he has had training. (All except so-called "natural born cutting horses" which stay supple regardless of the fact that they are broken and ridden.) Often in reining contests a horse is seen to fall when forced to turn suddenly. This is caused by the fact that he cannot change leads in the air and is not prepared for the sudden change of direction, whereupon if he had been taught to change in the air while galloping, he would properly brace himself and make the turn easily.

Many horses that have learned to change leads easily and quickly when brought to a walk for the change, do it easily on figure 8's at the first trial; so, test the horse *Change of* out starting on a large 8 and gradually getting *Leads at* smaller until he changes. If he refuess to change *the Gallop* and awkwardly cuts a large 8 while cantering on one certain lead, proceed as follows: Start him cantering on the *right* lead and circling to the *left*. This is known as a false lead. Cut the circles smaller and smaller until it is evident that the horse is having trouble keeping his feet. Then suddenly reverse the signal and give the signal for the left lead (use right leg and lift strongly on the left rein). He will seldom refuse to change. Canter a while on the left lead. Stop and repeat the process in the opposite direction. With several days' practice, gradually cutting the circles larger and larger, he may easily be made to change in the air on the straightaway. When he has reached this point in his training, there will be no trouble about his changing twice in reasonably small figure 8's, after which no attention need be paid to leads as the horse will change of his own accord to suit the occasion, just as the "natural cutting horse" changes without training.

At this point in training, it is a good idea to start working the horse at the canter through a set of about six stakes, increasing the speed as he becomes more proficient at doing a flying change of leads between the stakes as he changes directions. Use about six stakes and set them 16 feet apart. Walk and trot the horse through them a few times, weaving to the right of one and to the left of the next, to allow him to get the idea. Do not forget to use legs and body correctly as each change of direction is made. After he knows what is wanted, work at a slow canter, assisting with hands, legs, and body according to instructions already given to see that he makes the flying change between stakes. (By the term "flying change of leads" is meant a change of leads in the air as the horse gallops.) Keep increasing the speed of working and when he is running the course correctly and easily, begin setting him down in a sliding stop, according to instructions which will follow, at the end of the course and whirling him back on hind feet to run the course in the opposite direction. If your training up to this point has been thorough, he will make you ride to stay on him as he runs the course and whirls.

A horse trained up to this point is not a finished product but is really ready to go to work. Of course, the longer he is properly ridden, the better he responds to hands, legs, and body and, in time will almost work entirely on legs and body without reins. Many good, young horses make fine cutting horses that would otherwise become discouraged without preliminary training. Some will be just as good as the "naturals" but if they are put to work before they are taught to work on the haunches and to do a flying change of leads, they soon lose interest from heavy hands jerking on the bit and spurs gouging their sides in attempts to make them do what is impossible for them before being trained.

All through the training period, figure 8's are a valuable means of increasing suppleness. Cut them first at the walk, then at the trot, but never at the canter until the horse has first been taught the change of leads. Do not overdo figure 8's, nor any other exercise for that matter.

From the very beginning, no lesson should last until the horse resents the action of hands and legs. At the first sign of "souring," instruction should cease but the horse may be ridden longer in an ordinary manner. The average period for a lesson is about 45 minutes. Some horses will stand an hour, but many only 30 minutes. It is the tendency of the amateur to overdo training, so use much judgment. At the first sign of "souring," require one more movement, then end the lesson.

Do not expect a horse ever to become trained if, during the training period, you ride him out with other horses and enter races or practice fast reining or try to set him down in a sliding stop before he is ready for it. It is not objectionable to ride him with other horses in an ordinary manner while practicing good horsemanship but wait until he is thoroughly trained before attempting fast work or entering contests of any kind. A month's work can be spoiled in 15 minutes by such mistakes.

Allow no one else to ride a horse in training if you ever expect to finish him. While he is in the uncertain period of training, he is easily confused by anyone who uses hands and legs in a manner different from the way you use yours. While the horse is being trained, the future owner should also receive training in the proper use of hands, legs, and body lest all your hard work go for nought.

When the horse has been trained to this degree, it is a simple matter to have him "sit down" and stop on hind feet. *Stopping and Turning on Hind Feet* First begin practicing at the walk, then at the trot, then at the canter and gallop and finally at the run. All that is necessary is to suddenly

A correct sliding stop on hind feet. Horse and rider relaxed, nose down, reins slack.

lean the body backward, use the hands lightly on the reins, and almost at the same instant strongly close both legs. When the reins are fingered, and the body leaned backward, the chin of the horse comes "in" and he slows immediately. When the legs are closed, the hind feet are pushed under the body. With nose down, chin "in," and hind feet under the body, the horse is jammed together in one compact mass, and there is nothing else to do except to slide to a stop on hind feet. The exercise should not be rushed nor overdone. Be sure the horse is perfect at stopping at the slower gaits before practicing at the gallop and the run.

The horse has already been taught to always turn on hind feet when the hands and legs are used properly so nothing further need be said in this respect except to say that the more sudden and fast the turn, the farther backward the body should be leaned, and the more decisive the action of hands and legs; especially must the outside leg be held firmly while making the turn. By the constant proper use of the body and legs, a good horse soon learns to rein and turn completely and quickly without reins. This is not mere "talk." It works and works easily. Anyone can learn it who has patience and persistence and who loves a horse.

Horse that has been trained according to instructions in this book doing fast stop
and turn on hind feet.

Early in the course of the suppling exercises, it is well
to begin backing the horse. Being able to back well is a part
Backing   of suppleness. Proceed as follows and use the same
method on all horses. With the horse's head just
above level, close both legs until a hind foot is felt to leave
the ground; then release the calves, lean well backward and

So called "trainer" trying to *force* horse to turn

finger the reins. All horses that have not been spoiled about backing, will do so readily and the first time. Horses that have been spoiled willl resist, but after a few trials, will begin to back. On these horses, stronger use of both hands and legs is necessary.

At the first lesson in backing, require only two steps backward, and repeat only a couple of times. Next day require four steps, and so on, and soon the horse backs easily any reasonable distance. If, when the calves are released and the body leaned backward, strong pressure is maintained with the thighs while the reins are fingered the horse will soon back on the legs alone without reins.

When the horse learns to respond readily with the use of

one leg and move the haunches to the side when one leg only is used, he may be guided with the legs as he backs and may be backed through a set of stakes.

Backing is a valuable exercise in suppling if not over-done. Require the horse to back often and straight, gradually increasing the distance. If it is desired to later teach the horse rope work, each time he is backed the command "Back" should be repeated often.

After a horse has been suppled and made light and other-wise trained according to these instructions, it is a simple matter to teach him to work on a rope. A colt *Rope* broken by the methods outlined herein has no fear *Work* of a rope, even the first time it is swung from a saddle. A horse broken by other methods and that fears a rope when swung, may be easily changed in that respect by being worked on the longe line, taught to "freeze" at the command "Whoa," and a rope swung around and over him while keeping him stationary on a slack line as outlined under the instructions for breaking. When he will stand without excitement while working from the ground, mount and continue swinging the loop, requiring him to stand perfectly still on a slack rein. If he moves, jerk sufficiently hard, command "Whoa" and slack immediately. Keep swing-ing the rope. Great care should be taken not to let the rope hit the horse's head or ears while it is being swung. Should it brush him lightly on other parts of his body, he will soon learn that no harm is intended. After he has lost all fear of a swinging rope while standing, move him forward, and by using ordinary judgment, he loses all fear in a short time. Then begin throwing the rope out and dragging it in, using the same methods; pulling and slacking and commanding "Whoa" if he becomes excited. In two or three lessons he will lose all fear, if good judgment and firm methods are used.

To teach the horse to sit back on a rope and keep it tight, proceed as follows: shorten the bridle reins (snaffle) or hacka-more reins (By this time if you have trained according to in-structions, the horse will work equally well on either hacka-

Teaching Rope Work.

more or bridle and with either curb or snaffle bit) until they lack about eight inches of reaching the saddle horn. Place a fairly snug neck rope just back of the horse's ears. Run the end of the lariat backward through the neck rope and *through the fork of the saddle* from front to rear and *attach to the reins*. Mount and throw the lariat out on the ground, jump off, but not so fast as to excite the horse, step out in front and begin pulling and slacking on the rope, and repeating the command "Back" which you have already taught him from the saddle. He is confused at first, but with patience and some manipulation of the rope, he soon begins to back. Do not overdo it. Back him two or three times the first day and quit. Continue the lesson the next day, pulling and slacking less all the time, and soon he will back on command alone. If he happens to be slow in learning, *do not throw a loop in the rope to strike him on the nose*. Use patience and judgment until he learns what is wanted.

When he will back readily on command, attach a second rope to the saddle horn, first running it through the neck loop, and throw both ropes at once. Have a big, solid loop in the rope fastened to the saddle horn into which you can step and slide quickly up around the waist, being careful to see that the loop is big enough to allow you to get out of it easily in case of trouble. With loop around the waist and the other rope (the one fastened to the reins) in the hands, lie back on the loop and pull on the saddle horn, at the same time causing the horse with the other rope to back very slightly, or at least hold tight. When he will do this, suddenly slack on the rope around the waist, and work the other rope fast, as if you were in a great haste, causing him to back and take up the slack; at which time cease action on the rope in your hands, except to have him keep the other rope tight and perhaps back very slightly. Do not prolong a lesson until the horse is angry. A little practice each day over a number of days is much better than too much in one day. Continue this procedure until when you slack off on the loop around the waist and thus release tension on the saddle horn, the horse automatically runs swiftly backward to take up the slack.

By working often from the side, the horse soon learns to face in the direction of the loop.

When the horse has absolutely learned to keep the slack out of the rope on the saddle horn, the rope which is fastened to the reins may be dispensed with and a live calf may be roped. Remember when you set the horse down, do it according to previous instructions and *not by sudden and violent jerking on the reins.* He will slide easily and calmly to a stop *with nose down* and hind legs under body, and with no tossing of the head nor star-gazing. Jump off and stand at his head for a time, using the reins to see that he keeps the rope tight. The live calf will more or less excite him at first, but he soon learns to pay no attention to it, if you work calmly and sing or whistle as if such things are apt to happen almost any time. When he has quieted and is holding the calf on a tight rope, make the tie. Throw up the hands to indicate the tie is made. (The horse is watching) then step forward and begin to pull and slack on the rope, repeating the command "Come here," which you have taught him previously on the longe line, thus causing him to slack off. In a very few lessons he will go through the procedure automatically. If he begins to anticipate commands, and slacks off too quickly, it may be necessary to again attach the second rope to the reins, and correct it.

If, during the training period while using a live calf, the horse shows tendencies to bolt and run, correct him by banging the bosal of the hackamore across his nose and commanding "Whoa"; or even by the use of the running W.

After the foundation training, the horse has received in

How not to do it. Horse blind from pain in mouth caused by heavy hands jerking on bit, entire body rigid. This horse works from fear.

suppleness and lightness, training him to rope work is chiefly a matter of patience and judgment; but if you rush matters, get impatient and lose your temper, you will probably spoil a good horse. Much repetition is necessary. It is plain to be seen that the lessons in longeing and suppling must be completed before any of the end results are possible. *Do not make the mistake of starting in the middle of this course for anything. Start at the beginning or you will have no results whatever.*

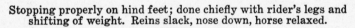

Stopping properly on hind feet; done chiefly with rider's legs and shifting of weight. Reins slack, nose down, horse relaxed.

Any horse that has been broken and handled according to the instructions under the section on breaking, will stand for mounting and will not go forward until the legs are closed against his sides, but it is necessary to continue mounting on a *slack* rein. Nearly all horses which are hard to mount have been made that way by mounting on a tight rein and thus jerking the mouth of the horse when the swing is made into the saddle.

Standing to Mount

If, under the stress of much excitement, a trained horse wants to move while you are attempting to mount, all that is necessary to have him stand quietly and forget the excitement is to jerk sharply on the reins, slack, and command "Whoa" as though you meant it.

In the case of a horse which has not been broken by the methods described herein, and which is hard to mount, it is an easy matter to change him in this respect. Merely put him on the longe line and teach him to "freeze" when the command "Whoa" is given (See the section on breaking). Each time he is stopped, run to him requiring him absolutely not to move and bang stirrup leathers, slap him under the belly, and make much commotion. Work from both sides. In fifteen minutes, begin inserting one foot in the stirrup, *always on a slack line*, and putting some weight in the stirrup, increasing the weight each time. If he moves, use the line to bang the bosal across his nose and the command "Whoa." Keep repeating until he absolutely stands on a slack line, and allows you to mount from either side. You may win a bet on horses hard to mount in 30 to 45 minutes, mounting from either side and leaving the reins on the ground.

Afterward, if ordinary judgment and manipulation are used and if mounting is done on a slack rein, the horse will continue to stand for mounting.

Never allow anyone to hold a horse for mounting. There is no better way to teach a fractious horse bad manners. Teach him to stand on a slack rein by the use of the longe line as detailed elsewhere in this book and there is seldom any trouble about mounting if you continue to do so on a slack rein.

Never snub a green horse to a saddle horn for mounting.

The system of breaking detailed in this book makes snubbing and leading unnecessary. The horse is bridle-wise and quiet before he is mounted. The first time he is mounted, it is not objectionable of an assistant on foot in the corral leads him the first few steps on a slack line, helping to stop him if there is excitement, but even this should not be necessary more than a time or two. It takes only a few minutes to teach him to go forward when squeezed with the legs. Bridle-wising the colt on foot in the corral before mounting is as important, if not more so, than teaching him not to fear you.

The best advice on teaching ground tying to horses used chiefly for pleasure in thickly populated districts is, "Don't do it." In early days on the range, when people and
Ground Tying horses were scarce and there were no automobiles, the horse often learned it himself. The rider dropped the reins and if the horse moved he stepped on them, and soon threw up his head, which jerked him violently. He soon learned not to move when the reins were down. Often hobbles were used to be sure he did not get away. In either case, there was not continued excitement to cause him to want to move as there is today. At that, most horses of early days eventually found that they could move and graze by turning their heads to one side so as not to step on the reins. The remark was often heard, "That horse can run faster with his reins dragging, than he can when after a cow." However, if you *must* teach your horse to stand with reins on the ground, and take the chance of injuring a sensitive mouth, which so far you have protected, proceed as follows: Each time you stop and dismount, hobble the horse and drop the reins. When he stands well, after a few weeks of practice, adjust both sides of the hobble on the same leg for a few lessons. Then remove the hobbles entirely. Do not be in too much of a hurry to discontinue hobbling.

Or, a different method, and one successfully used, is that of burying around a pasture of several acres, logs or other objects with chain and snap attached, the snap above the ground, deep enough and strong enough that the horse cannot pull them out when and if he "sits back" on the halter or hackamore when the snap is attached to the reins or lead rope. Place a strong ring in the hackamore rein or lead rope, which should also be strong, and ride to a spot where a log is buried. Dismount quickly and drop both bridle and hackamore reins, quickly fasten the ring in the hackamore reins to the snap fastened to the log, and leave the immediate vicinity. Usually there is a fight for a few seconds, even in a horse well halter broken, but it does not last long. If he is not well halter broken, the fight may be serious, and may even result in an injured horse.

Leave the horse a matter of fifteen minutes and again ride around the pasture several times, and tie in another location. Each time, act as though you were in a hurry but make no move to scare the horse. When he will stand well and indefinitely in the pasture, repeat the process outside a time or two, and he is pretty well broken for ground tying. However, in time he will usually learn that he can move when the reins are dropped in this age of noise and excitement.

Absolutely the most important part of this course and the substance of it, is that part dealing with suppling and making the horse light. When this has been *Lofty Action for Parades* accomplished, teaching other things is an easy matter. It may require a long time, sometimes months, or you may see results very quickly. Do not begin training for anything except the walk, trot, and fox-trot until you are sure the horse is supple and light.

After the horse has been suppled and made light if high, slow action is wanted, use the legs strongly and use the hands enough to prevent fast forward movement. The horse uses the increased propulsion caused by the use of the rider's legs in high action because excessive forward movement is prevented by the hands on the reins. In order to obtain this lofty action, the horse must absolutely be light with all that the word implies and should have been in training many months before it is attempted. If started too soon, he will soon "sour."

Another method, although mechanical, and one which may be used along with the one just described is as follows: Each horse has a spot on each front leg which, if touched, will cause him to raise the leg. It is somewhere between the body and the fetlock. Stand at the right shoulder of the horse facing his body, raise the head by means of a snaffle, and push most of his weight onto the left leg; then begin to lightly tap the right leg of the horse with the quirt until you find this spot. When he raises his leg in any manner, cease action immediately, and let him know he has done the right thing. Repeat. Go to the left side and obtain the same results reversing the procedure, of course. Do not expect too much. If the legs are raised in any manner during the first lesson, you should be satisfied. Practice only a few minutes each day until the legs are raised high. Soon after he starts raising the legs, begin using slight action on the rein on the side on which you are working. Soon he will raise the leg high when you use the rein and point the quirt at the leg. This is the time at which you should mount and begin practicing from the saddle. First, by use of the reins and quirt, require him to raise the legs high while standing, and when he will do this, crowd him slowly forward with the legs, making certain that he does not get the habit of raising one leg high for a step and slighting the movement with the other. In this work, strict attention should be paid to diagonal horsemanship—left leg, right rein; right leg, left rein.

When the horse will do a slow, high walk of even cadence, start increasing the speed slowly. Do not rush him. Later he will trot high, exaggerating his action. Not less than two months should be required to teach good, high exaggerated action. *Unless the horse is first made supple and light*, according to directions previously given, he will never be proficient at the high walk and trot, nor in any other movement, for that matter.

Although this course is not intended to deal with hunters and jumpers, any good square-gaited saddle horse should
Jumping be taught to easily clear obstacles up to $3\frac{1}{2}$ feet in height. If he can do this, he can also clear ordinary

obstacles that require a broad jump, such as ditches and coulees.

When the horse has been trained according to the instructions in this course, and is a good riding horse or a good stock horse, begin putting him over poles lying on the ground, first, at the walk, then at the trot, and finally, at the canter. In a few days, raise the poles to a height of 8 inches. Do not require more than four jumps in one lesson. If you push him too fast, he will soon start refusing. As you progress, gradually raise the poles 4 to 6 inches at a time, until he is clearing them at 3½ feet. After you have the height at 18 inches, do the work at a canter. Do not allow the horse to acquire the habit of rushing a jump. With a well suppled horse, this is easy to prevent. Start cantering slowly towards the obstacles, and when about 4 strides from it, give him his head and let him speed. If he acquires the habit of waiting for the take-off until he is too close to the obstacles, place a pole or bar on the ground in front of it; two feet away when the jump is two feet high, three feet away when it is three and one-half feet high. This will force him to take off at the proper distance.

In jumping horses, there are a few things which are important to remember. First, *you cannot help the horse over a jump.* Merely see that you do not hinder him by riding the reins or by improper body balance. Let him take the jump on a slack rein. Imagine yourself taking a jump with someone pulling on a bit in your mouth. Do not believe the oft-repeated statement that you can or should "lift" the horse over the jump. Ride forward with heels well down and back of perpendicular and body leaning over the horse's withers. As he takes the jump, ride the stirrups for the most part; "float" on the saddle. He will not strike your face with his head. When a horse jumps, his withers raise, but his head goes down. As the horse goes over the jump, your body should straighten but not so much that when the fore feet strike the ground, your back is at right angles to the back of the horse.

Second, do not "grab" the horse with the bit the second he lands. Gradually ease him into it in two or three strides

No horsemanship is being used here. This sketch was made from photograph of man said to be "training" the horse to do a sliding stop. If instructions in this book are followed you will not be caught in an act like this.

after landing; being "grabbed" makes him dread the jump, and soon he will be refusing, if you keep it up.

Third, when teaching him to jump, never use obstacles which will fall at a touch, if he does not make the jump well. Arrange them solidly. Let him bark his shins a time or two and stumble and he will learn to clear the obstacles each time, instead of getting in the habit of knocking them down.

If you do not jump him too much and too often, he will perhaps tick and stumble a time or two, then clear the obstacles in good form every time. If you do jump him too much and too often, he may begin refusing, or get into a state of mind in which he cares little if he does fall; in which case you have probably ruined your horse for jumping.

The method just described for teaching your horse to jump a little for ordinary riding, may not be altogether the best method for training hunters and jumpers.

TRAINING THE CUTTING HORSE

As has been said before, a natural cutting horse is merely a horse that has it in him to like to work cattle, that stays supple and light, works from the haunches, and retains the ability to do a flying change of leads in spite of being mounted and broken. When you have taught almost any good young horse these things before working him on cattle and making him still stiffer in his movements and putting him in a frame of mind in which he does not want to work cattle, he will usually take to the work as if it were a game you are teaching him to play. Some will not do this. These horses simply seem not to be interested in cattle, very much like a person who cannot make himself like cards—or horses. This can be determined in half a dozen trials or lessons at working cattle. If he is one of those which shows no interest and hands, legs, and body must continue to be used to have him turn and twist in handling a single animal, it is best not to continue to try to make of him a top cutting horse. If the horse, however, after a few trials, shows signs of taking an interest in the work, and most good horses will, he will almost learn it by himself if you do not push him too fast. The whole idea is to have him learn to "work on his own" and without the use of the aids of the rider, just as the natural cutting horse works. He will do this just as soon as he gets the idea of what is wanted. To give him this idea it is necessary at first to use legs and body, and hands to some extent, when you want him to turn a cow. Needless to say, if your training has been thorough, the horse by this time always turns on hind feet by the use of the body and legs and with very little use of the reins.

When starting to train a horse for cutting cattle, after he has first been suppled and made light and taught to work from the haunches and do a flying change of leads, it is best to hold the herd of cattle in a small enclosure and turn only one in the larger corral or arena. If, when you are slowly pushing the animal away from the herd, she suddenly turns and gets by the horse, there is not so much confusion as there is when she can rejoin the herd and the horse does not become discouraged so easily. Work slowly at first, chiefly at a walk, and stay at quite a distance from the cow. When she turns and tries to get back to the herd, the horse does not have to turn and dodge as fast as if he were close up. At first, use legs and body (and the reins as little as possible) in an effort to have the horse dodge with the cow and prevent her from getting back. Always have the horse turn and dodge with his head to the cow. Never allow him to turn with head away from cow. If she gets by, and she will at first, stay cool and calm and do not *chase* her back to the end of the corral or arena. Walk, trot, or canter slowly back, get around the cow and start again. Repeat this performance only a few times in a lesson. Do not keep it up until the horse is tired. It is just a matter of a few lessons until the horse will "work on his own" and all you will need to do is RIDE. As he becomes more proficient, he will, of his own accord, work closer to the cow. Soon the herd may be turned into the corral or arena and held by an assistant, and the horse given practice in nosing a single animal out and taking her away.

In riding a good cutting horse, it is very necessary that you ride well and correctly according to instructions already given. Ride "down and forward" in the saddle and turn with the horse and by no means interfere with him by using the reins.

A cutting horse trained in this manner will compete favorably with any natural cutting horse. The fundamental training in suppleness, lightness, and the flying change of leads has "paid off."

LEARNING TO RIDE A BUCKING HORSE

While being able to ride a bucking horse does not make a horseman of you, being able to sit well in a saddle is a necessary part of good horsemanship and the better you can sit, the better you can focus your attention upon the training and handling of your horse because you do not have to worry about staying on the horse at times of argument or excitement. Also, it is a pleasure and satisfaction to be able to sit well and to enter contests when the occasion arises.

Many people ride all their lives and never learn to balance themselves on a rough horse. Many cow hands do a top notch job of working cattle with a well-broken horse but are thrown by the poorest bucker. Most of these people try to brace themselves by thrusting their feet forward in the stirrups and sitting back on the loins of the horse. As has been previously explained, this is exactly the wrong thing to do unless you are strong enough to hold yourself on the horse by sheer grip of the legs and by riding the halter, hackamore, or bridle reins at the same time and this kind of riding is no credit to you.

If you are young and have practiced and learned the method of riding advocated in this course in horsemanship (See section on Riding) until you can gallop a good horse down the side of a steep, rough hill and remain well balanced in the saddle or can take jumps of five feet without trouble, you can learn to ride a bucking horse by practicing riding a good horse over jumps of three feet placed close enough together that the horse does not have room between jumps to do more than make a catch step before he springs for the next jump. The height of the jumps and the distance between them will vary with the conformation and the jumping ability of the horse. A little practice with each horse will tell you. The number of jumps will vary also but about four is a good number after you have practiced awhile with two. Needless to say, you should have enough consideration for the horse not to overdo the practice at any one time. Stop immediately if you see the horse is tired of the game.

When you have become proficient enough that you can sit a good horse over half a dozen jumps placed close together and as high as he can take them springing immediately from one jump to the next, you are ready to try the real thing and will probably sit all right if the horse is not too good at the game. From there on out, practice is the main thing and in time you will learn good balance and learn to be quick in changing the position of your body to correspond to the movements of the horse. This is necessary when riding "sunfishers" and "spinners" or even when riding a good cutting horse in action.

After learning good balance and quickness of movement with the proper seat, with still more practice you will work out a system of your own if you want to scratch the horse with the spurs as is required in rodeo performances.

ADVANCED WORK ON THE LONGE LINE

The chief use of the longe line in breaking and training stock horses is in teaching obedience according to the methods already described in detail in this course. Use of it, however, can go much farther if the trainer wishes and has the time to devote to such use. Much work on the longe line is advisable in colts too young to be ridden, in spoiled horses, and in horses whose backs have been injured so that they should not be ridden for awhile. Also, when the trainer is temporarily unable to ride, much may be accomplished with the longe line. Some trainers will use it a great deal more than others. Personally, I can do much more toward suppling and making the horse light by working from his back. No matter what you teach on the longe line you must still teach it again when mounted but of course it will come much easier if the work on the longe has been thorough. Before going into advanced work on the longe line, first teach the horse an extended walk, trot, and gallop, using the hackamore or an ordinary snaffle bridle and keeping him at the end of a line about 30 feet in length. Teach him to do these gaits and to stop or come to you upon command as detailed under the section on Breaking.

For advanced work on the longe line a surcingle with crupper and the necessary rings is needed; also, a longeing bridle, the reins of which pass through rings in the headstall near the ears of the horse and fasten to the side rings of the surcingle. This is for the purpose of teaching the horse to carry his head up. Side reins also run from the bit, which should be a snaffle, to the surcingle and are adjusted at first so that there is only slight pressure on the horse's mouth as he is longed. Gradually these reins are shortened until he carries his head with forehead almost perpendicular. Some horses learn sooner than others that if they flex their necks at the poll and relax the muscles of the lower jaw, pressure on their mouths is relieved. If the side reins contain pieces of strong elastic, their action will more nearly simulate the action of good hands, although it is never possible to entirely reach this goal with any mechanical contrivance.

While the horse is learning to "give" to the bit and flex his neck at the poll, he should be made to keep his hind feet well under the body as he travels and should gradually be slowed at the trot and the canter while maintaining good action with his feet and legs. As he learns and improves, the longe line should be shortened gradually until he is doing a good high, slow trot and a slow canter with good action on a very short line. Securing the same performance when mounted is then the matter of a short time.

For advanced lessons on the longe line, a longeing whip should be used. The stock of such a whip is usually four feet in length and the lash is 11 or 12 feet. Such a whip and also the necessary bridle and surcingle may be obtained from various firms which handle riding and training equipment. With yourself in the center of the circle, as the horse moves around you, keep him enclosed between the line in front and the whip behind, the horse forming the base of a triangle, yourself the point, and the line and whip forming the sides. When the whip is in the rear of the horse, it should signify that he is to go forward; when it is moved up along his side, it means that he should slow and when pointing in front of his chest, he should stop. To execute a change of hand (reverse the direction of moving) while in motion, if the horse is going to the left, change the rein to the right hand in which is held the whip, pull lightly on the line, step forward and hold out left hand in front of moving horse, keeping him in motion with the whip. He will become excited at first because he does not know what you want but soon will pass in front of you; at which time the whip should be shifted to the left hand and the horse kept moving. If he is cantering or galloping, he must also change from right to left lead and soon learns to do it easily. As can easily be seen, a fairly good walk, trot, and canter and the flying change of leads may be taught by correct use of the longe line.

No matter what you want to teach your horse, start

reading and following this course from the beginning. Do not try to begin elsewhere. The horse must absolutely be suppled and made light before he can be trained properly for anything else. Read and re-read. Study and review. Repeat! Repeat! Repeat!